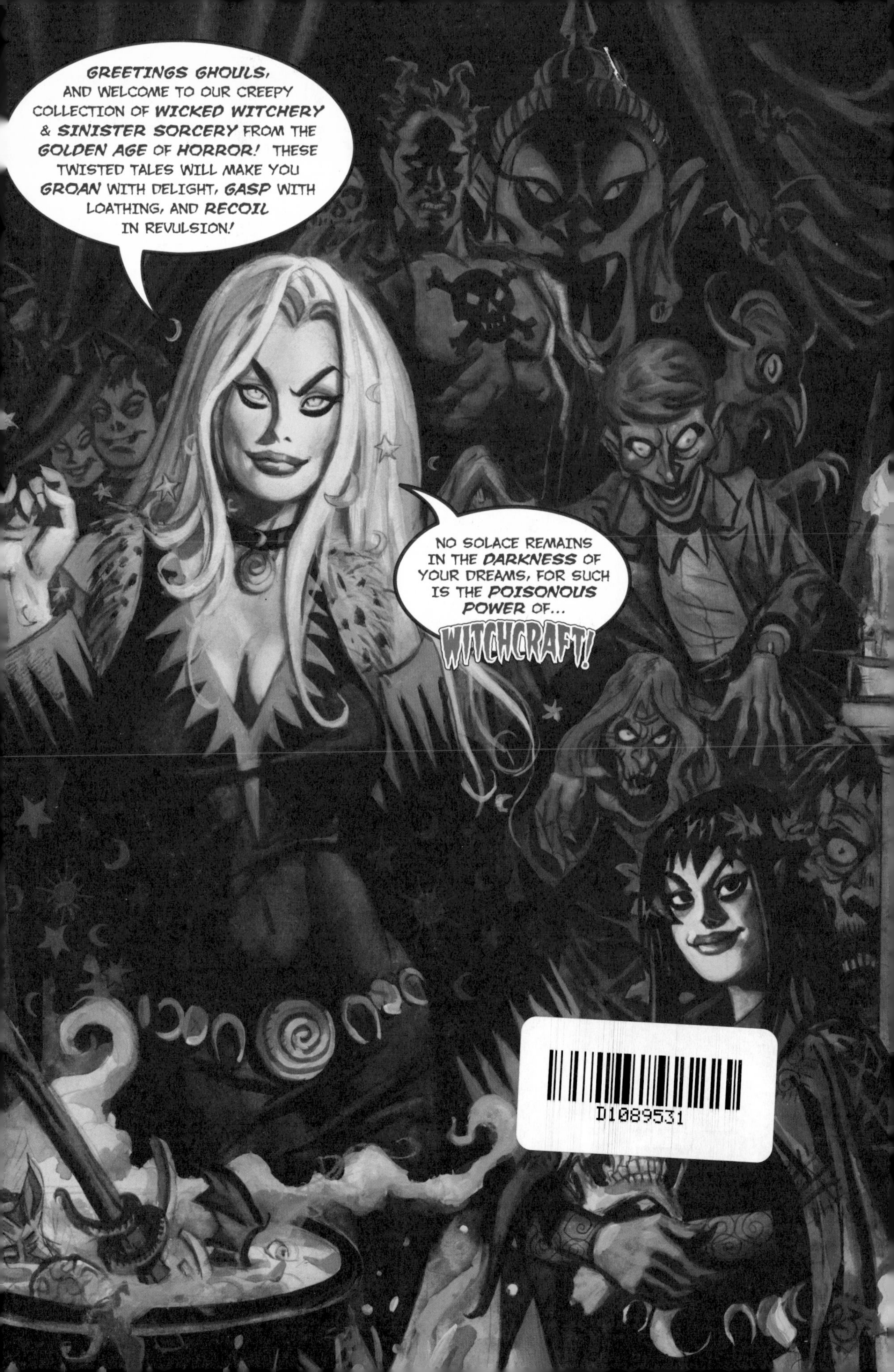
GREETINGS GHOULS, AND WELCOME TO OUR CREEPY COLLECTION OF WICKED WITCHERY & SINISTER SORCERY FROM THE GOLDEN AGE OF HORROR! THESE TWISTED TALES WILL MAKE YOU GROAN WITH DELIGHT, GASP WITH LOATHING, AND RECOIL IN REVULSION!
NO SOLACE REMAINS IN THE DARKNESS OF YOUR DREAMS, FOR SUCH IS THE POISONOUS POWER OF...
WITCHCRAFT!
D1089531

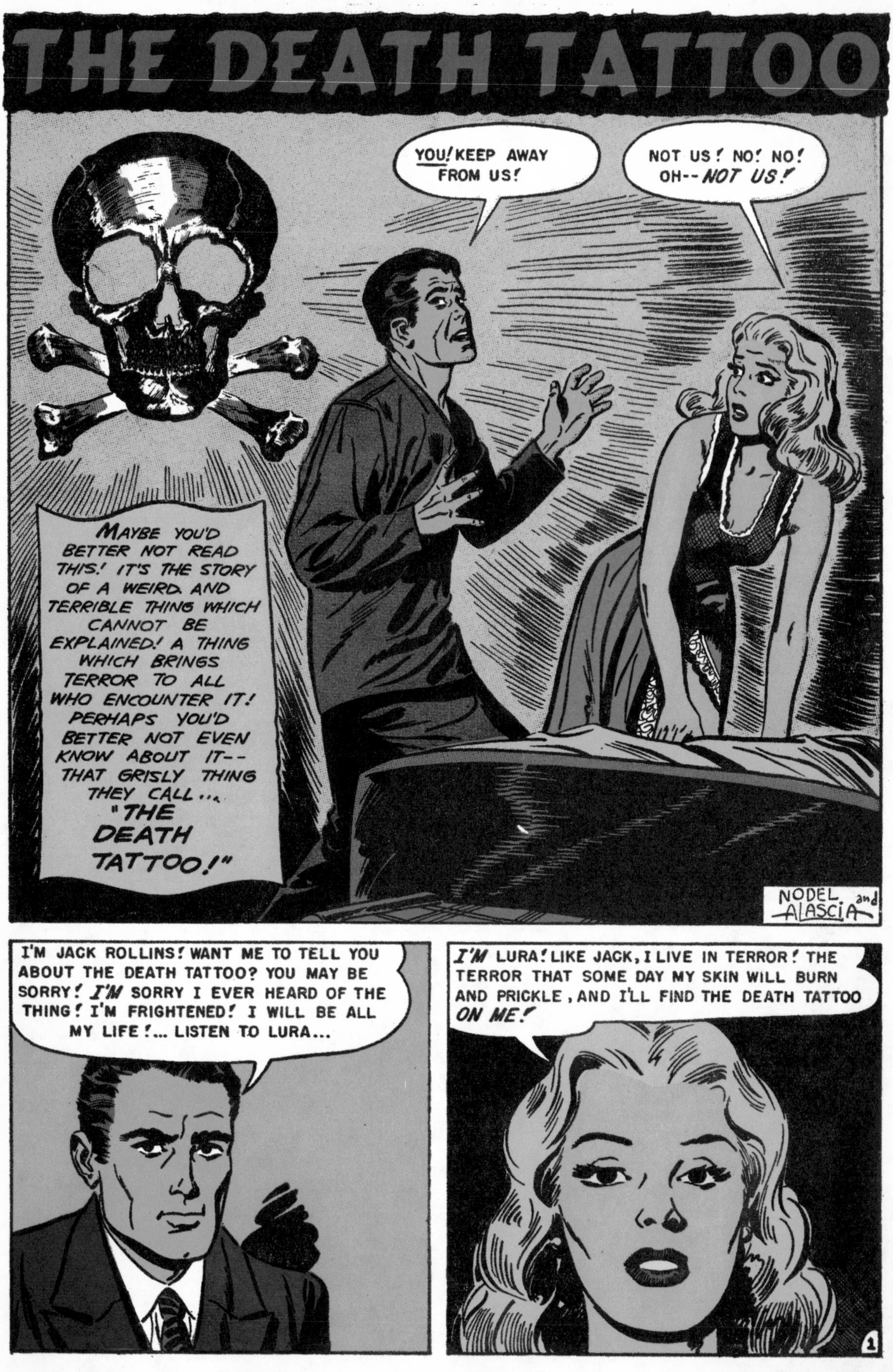
THE DEATH TATTOO
YOU! KEEP AWAY FROM US!
NOT US! NO! NO! OH-- NOT US!
MAYBE YOU'D BETTER NOT READ THIS! IT'S THE STORY OF A WEIRD AND TERRIBLE THING WHICH CANNOT BE EXPLAINED! A THING WHICH BRINGS TERROR TO ALL WHO ENCOUNTER IT! PERHAPS YOU'D BETTER NOT EVEN KNOW ABOUT IT-- THAT GRISLY THING THEY CALL... "THE DEATH TATTOO!"
NODEL and ALASCIA
I'M JACK ROLLINS! WANT ME TO TELL YOU ABOUT THE DEATH TATTOO? YOU MAY BE SORRY! I'M SORRY I EVER HEARD OF THE THING! I'M FRIGHTENED! I WILL BE ALL MY LIFE!... LISTEN TO LURA...
I'M LURA! LIKE JACK, I LIVE IN TERROR! THE TERROR THAT SOME DAY MY SKIN WILL BURN AND PRICKLE, AND I'LL FIND THE DEATH TATTOO ON ME!
1

IT BEGAN FOR ME THE DAY I APPLIED FOR A JOB WITH APEC'S CARNIVAL!

I'M A CONTORTIONIST! MR. APEC, I'M GOOD! JUST GIVE ME A TRY, YOU'LL SEE!

A CONTORTIONIST? WELL, ALL RIGHT, I'LL TRY YOU!

MY ACT GOT APPLAUSE! APEC KEPT ME...

SAY, HE SURE CAN TWIST HIMSELF UP, CAN'T HE?

HE'S GOOD!

IT WAS A THIRD-RATE TENT SHOW...THE PUBLIC CALLED MY FELLOW PERFORMERS "FREAKS"..BUT THEY WERE JUST REGULAR PEOPLE, LIKE EVERYBODY ELSE!

YOUR ACT'S NOT BAD AT ALL, YOUNG MAN!

THANKS!

THAT'S HOW I MET LURA! SHE WAS ASSISTANT TO PROFESSOR GARTH...THE HYPNOTIST...

THIS IS LURA...NICEST OF THE BUNCH!

WELL! THANKS, WILLIE!

NO ARGUMENT ON THAT!

PROFESSOR GARTH'S HYPNOTIST ACT WAS OUR HEADLINER! THE THING GAVE...EVEN ME, A PERFORMER... THE CREEPS!

YOU'RE POWERLESS AGAINST ME! YOU WILL DO MY BIDDING!

YES! OH, YES!

NOW, WHO WANTS TO TRY BEING HYPNOTIZED? I OFFER ONE HUNDRED DOLLARS TO ANYONE WHO CAN WITHSTAND MY COMMANDS!

NOT ME... UGH!...

2

OCCASIONALLY SOMEBODY ACCEPTED, BUT HE NEVER HAD TO PAY THE MONEY! COULD HE REALLY HYP-NOTIZE PEOPLE?

YOU'RE POWER-LESS AGAINST ME!

DOES THAT FELLOW REALLY HAVE HYPNOTIC POWER?

SEARCH ME! I DON'T WANT ANY PART OF HIM!

ME NEITHER! UGH!

GARTH KEPT TO HIMSELF! NOBODY LIKED HIM!

I WOULDN'T WANT HIM MAD AT ME! WHY LURA WORKS FOR HIM IS A MYSTERY!

HE'S SURE QUEER!

AND THERE WAS SOMETHING QUEER ABOUT LURA! SOME-TIMES, BETWEEN SHOWS, I'D SEE...

...JUST SITTING, STARING! SHE LOOKS FRIGHTENED...TERRIFIED!

ONE NIGHT I SPOKE TO HER ABOUT IT, AND...

LURA...WHAT'S THE MATTER WITH YOU? ARE YOU AFRAID OF GARTH?

NO! NO...OH, DON'T ASK ME! I...I CAN'T TALK ABOUT IT! LET ME ALONE!

GARTH, HIMSELF, FREELY ADMITTED THAT HE WAS A FAKE! JUST A CLEVER SHOWMAN!

SO I'VE GOT YOU PEOPLE FOOLED, TOO! HA! HA! THAT'S GOOD!

I WAS WITH LURA A LOT DURING THAT WESTERN TRIP! AND ONE DAY...

LURA, I...I GUESS I'M FALLING IN LOVE WITH YOU! LURA, DEAR...

OHHH...?!

LURA, DARLING...LET'S GET MARRIED! I DO LOVE YOU! I DO!

NO! NO! OH, JACK...!

3

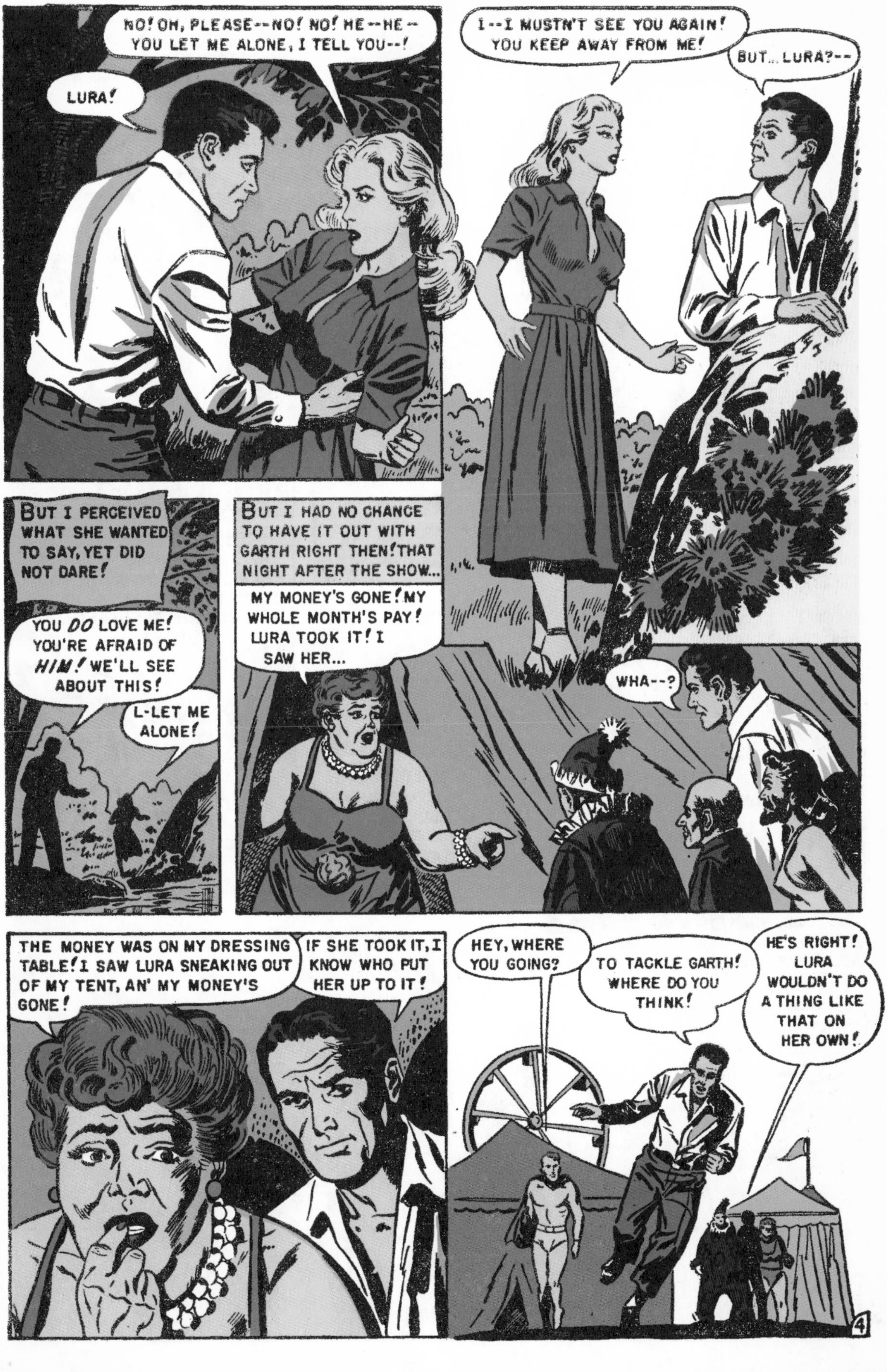

NO! OH, PLEASE--NO! NO! HE--HE--YOU LET ME ALONE, I TELL YOU--!
LURA!
I--I MUSTN'T SEE YOU AGAIN! YOU KEEP AWAY FROM ME!
BUT... LURA?--
BUT I PERCEIVED WHAT SHE WANTED TO SAY, YET DID NOT DARE!
YOU DO LOVE ME! YOU'RE AFRAID OF HIM! WE'LL SEE ABOUT THIS!
L-LET ME ALONE!
BUT I HAD NO CHANCE TO HAVE IT OUT WITH GARTH RIGHT THEN! THAT NIGHT AFTER THE SHOW...
MY MONEY'S GONE! MY WHOLE MONTH'S PAY! LURA TOOK IT! I SAW HER...
WHA--?
THE MONEY WAS ON MY DRESSING TABLE! I SAW LURA SNEAKING OUT OF MY TENT, AN' MY MONEY'S GONE!
IF SHE TOOK IT, I KNOW WHO PUT HER UP TO IT!
HEY, WHERE YOU GOING?
TO TACKLE GARTH! WHERE DO YOU THINK!
HE'S RIGHT! LURA WOULDN'T DO A THING LIKE THAT ON HER OWN!
4

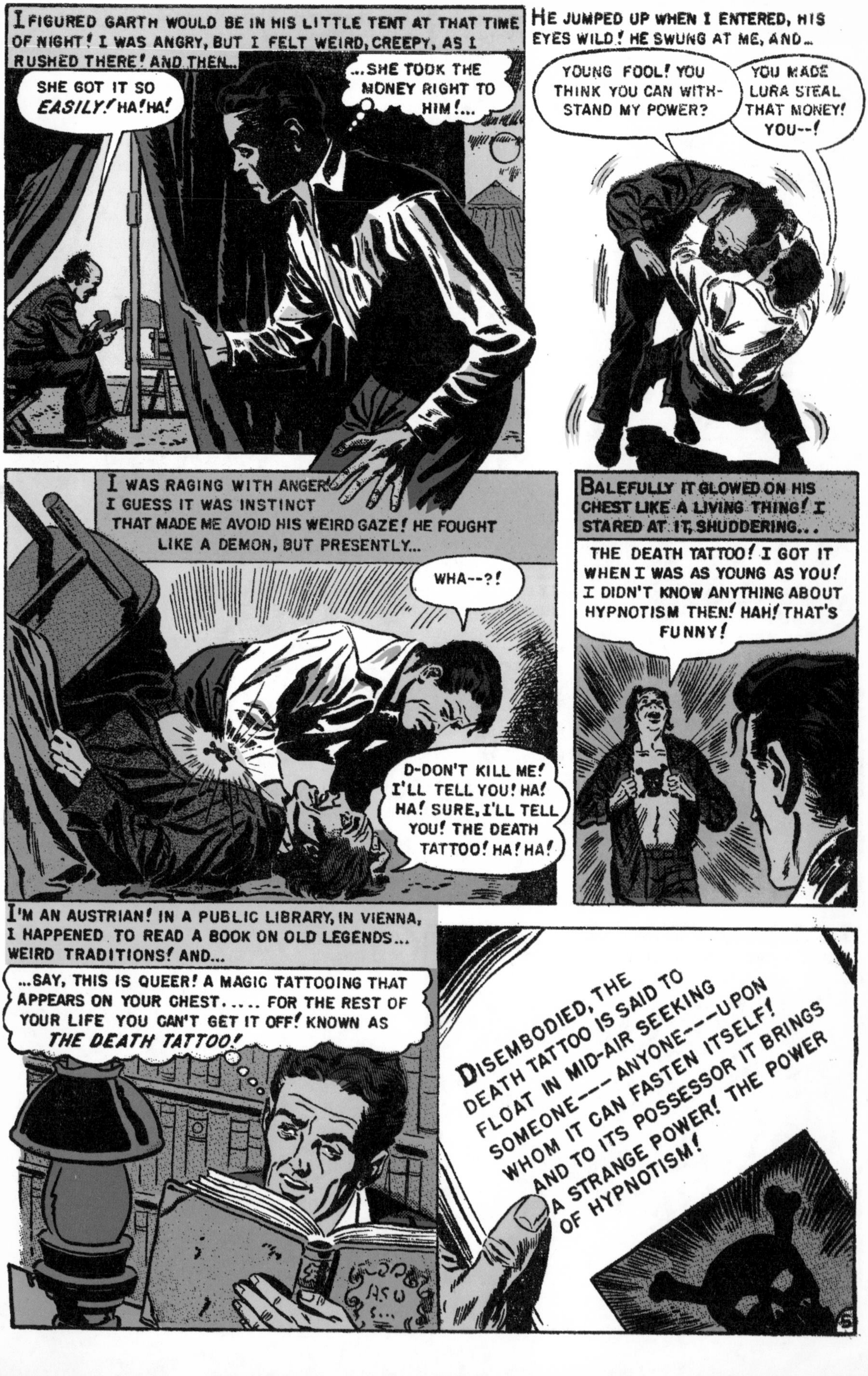
I FIGURED GARTH WOULD BE IN HIS LITTLE TENT AT THAT TIME OF NIGHT! I WAS ANGRY, BUT I FELT WEIRD, CREEPY, AS I RUSHED THERE! AND THEN...
SHE GOT IT SO EASILY! HA! HA!
...SHE TOOK THE MONEY RIGHT TO HIM!...
HE JUMPED UP WHEN I ENTERED, HIS EYES WILD! HE SWUNG AT ME, AND...
YOUNG FOOL! YOU THINK YOU CAN WITHSTAND MY POWER?
YOU MADE LURA STEAL THAT MONEY! YOU--!
I WAS RAGING WITH ANGER! I GUESS IT WAS INSTINCT THAT MADE ME AVOID HIS WEIRD GAZE! HE FOUGHT LIKE A DEMON, BUT PRESENTLY...
WHA--?!
D-DON'T KILL ME! I'LL TELL YOU! HA! HA! SURE, I'LL TELL YOU! THE DEATH TATTOO! HA! HA!
BALEFULLY IT GLOWED ON HIS CHEST LIKE A LIVING THING! I STARED AT IT, SHUDDERING...
THE DEATH TATTOO! I GOT IT WHEN I WAS AS YOUNG AS YOU! I DIDN'T KNOW ANYTHING ABOUT HYPNOTISM THEN! HAH! THAT'S FUNNY!
I'M AN AUSTRIAN! IN A PUBLIC LIBRARY, IN VIENNA, I HAPPENED TO READ A BOOK ON OLD LEGENDS... WEIRD TRADITIONS! AND...
...SAY, THIS IS QUEER! A MAGIC TATTOOING THAT APPEARS ON YOUR CHEST..... FOR THE REST OF YOUR LIFE YOU CAN'T GET IT OFF! KNOWN AS THE DEATH TATTOO!
DISEMBODIED, THE DEATH TATTOO IS SAID TO FLOAT IN MID-AIR SEEKING SOMEONE--- ANYONE---UPON WHOM IT CAN FASTEN ITSELF! AND TO ITS POSSESSOR IT BRINGS A STRANGE POWER! THE POWER OF HYPNOTISM!

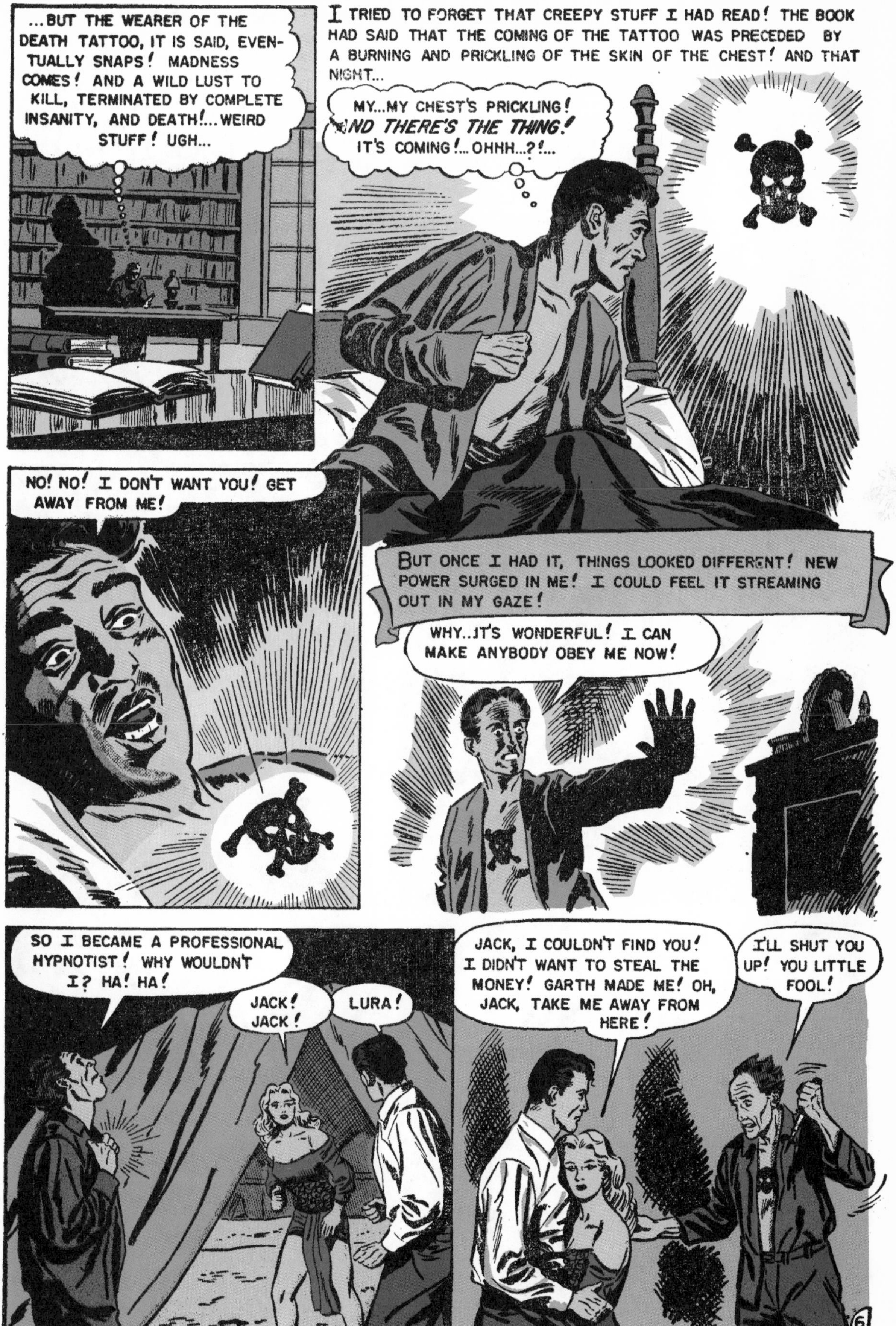
...BUT THE WEARER OF THE DEATH TATTOO, IT IS SAID, EVENTUALLY SNAPS! MADNESS COMES! AND A WILD LUST TO KILL, TERMINATED BY COMPLETE INSANITY, AND DEATH!...WEIRD STUFF! UGH...
I TRIED TO FORGET THAT CREEPY STUFF I HAD READ! THE BOOK HAD SAID THAT THE COMING OF THE TATTOO WAS PRECEDED BY A BURNING AND PRICKLING OF THE SKIN OF THE CHEST! AND THAT NIGHT...
MY...MY CHEST'S PRICKLING! AND THERE'S THE THING! IT'S COMING!...OHHH...?!...
NO! NO! I DON'T WANT YOU! GET AWAY FROM ME!
BUT ONCE I HAD IT, THINGS LOOKED DIFFERENT! NEW POWER SURGED IN ME! I COULD FEEL IT STREAMING OUT IN MY GAZE!
WHY..IT'S WONDERFUL! I CAN MAKE ANYBODY OBEY ME NOW!
SO I BECAME A PROFESSIONAL HYPNOTIST! WHY WOULDN'T I? HA! HA!
JACK! JACK!
LURA!
JACK, I COULDN'T FIND YOU! I DIDN'T WANT TO STEAL THE MONEY! GARTH MADE ME! OH, JACK, TAKE ME AWAY FROM HERE!
I'LL SHUT YOU UP! YOU LITTLE FOOL!
6

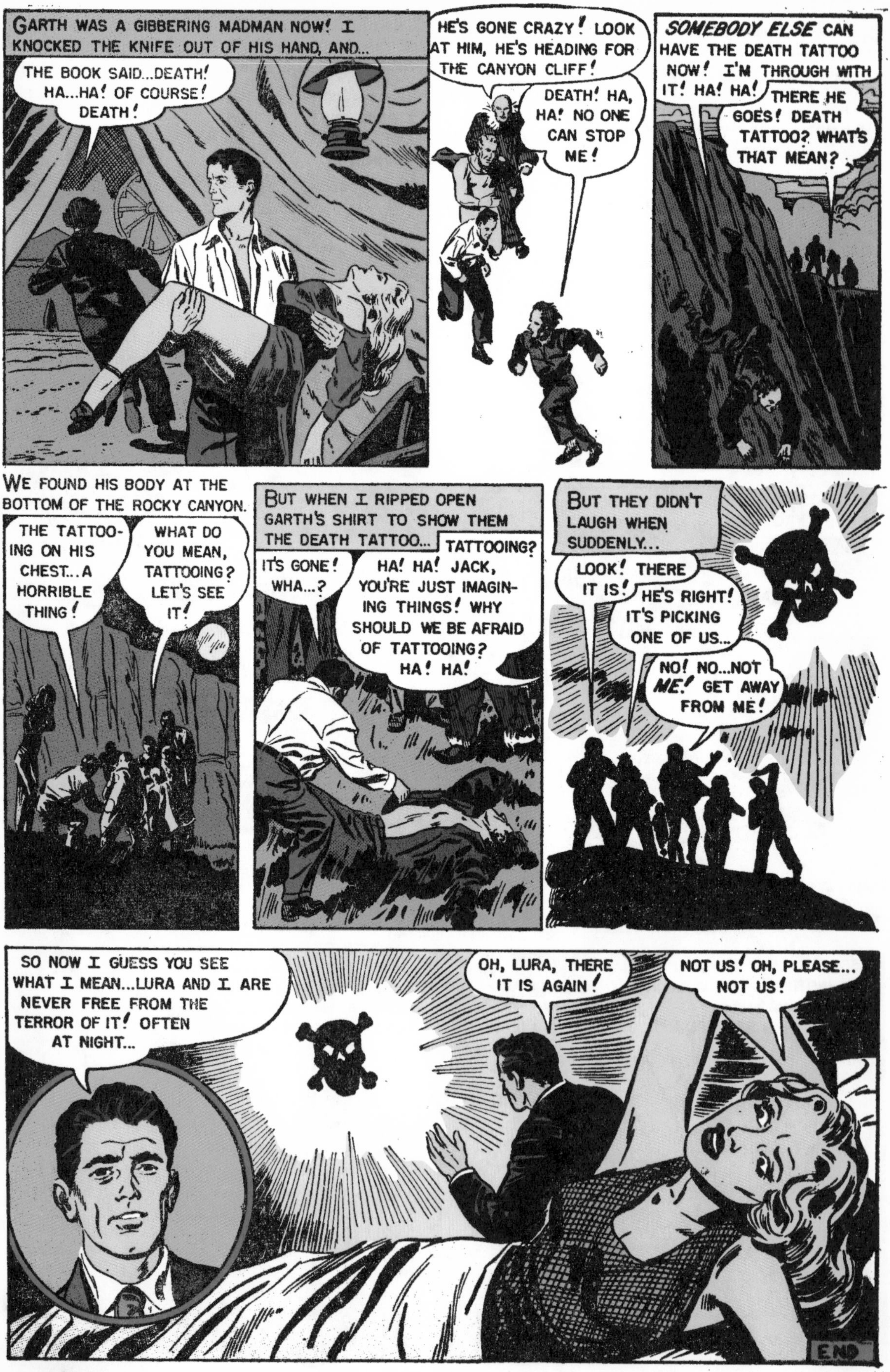
GARTH WAS A GIBBERING MADMAN NOW! I KNOCKED THE KNIFE OUT OF HIS HAND, AND...
THE BOOK SAID...DEATH! HA...HA! OF COURSE! DEATH!
HE'S GONE CRAZY! LOOK AT HIM, HE'S HEADING FOR THE CANYON CLIFF!
DEATH! HA, HA! NO ONE CAN STOP ME!
SOMEBODY ELSE CAN HAVE THE DEATH TATTOO NOW! I'M THROUGH WITH IT! HA! HA!
THERE HE GOES! DEATH TATTOO? WHAT'S THAT MEAN?
WE FOUND HIS BODY AT THE BOTTOM OF THE ROCKY CANYON.
THE TATTOO-ING ON HIS CHEST...A HORRIBLE THING!
WHAT DO YOU MEAN, TATTOOING? LET'S SEE IT!
BUT WHEN I RIPPED OPEN GARTH'S SHIRT TO SHOW THEM THE DEATH TATTOO...
IT'S GONE! WHA...?
TATTOOING? HA! HA! JACK, YOU'RE JUST IMAGIN-ING THINGS! WHY SHOULD WE BE AFRAID OF TATTOOING? HA! HA!
BUT THEY DIDN'T LAUGH WHEN SUDDENLY...
LOOK! THERE IT IS!
HE'S RIGHT! IT'S PICKING ONE OF US...
NO! NO...NOT ME! GET AWAY FROM ME!
SO NOW I GUESS YOU SEE WHAT I MEAN...LURA AND I ARE NEVER FREE FROM THE TERROR OF IT! OFTEN AT NIGHT...
OH, LURA, THERE IT IS AGAIN!
NOT US! OH, PLEASE... NOT US!
END

Is a dying curse powerful enough to destroy those who deserve it? Three people did not think so. They sat back, smug and content, secure in their knowledge of a murder that could never be traced--until a thing of utter evil--a creature from a rotted crypt, faced them with gloating laughter!

The VAMPIRE PUPPET

I HAVE COME FOR YOU, MARION--*FOR YOU!* HA, HA, HA...

N-NO! DON'T TOUCH ME! AIIIIIEEEEE!

In the small province of Bithnia, near the Mediterranean, there was a kindly, old puppeteer named Jacques Gravon. He was to all appearances a success...

BOW TO THE AUDIENCE NOW, KOKO! BOW!

MARVELOUS! BRAVO, KOKO! KOKO!

But it was really Koko, the puppet, who was the success. Koko, you see, had been recently made from shiny oak-wood and bright-colored bits of cloth. His humorous appearance drew crowds like a magnet...

AH--THAT LITTLE ONE IS VERY FUNNY! HA, HA... KOKO--KOKO!!

HERE IS A GOLD PIECE, KOKO! IT IS YOURS!

BUT MARION LEBLANCH, HER HUSBAND, HENRY, AND HER BROTHER, GEORGE, THE PUPPET ASSISTANTS, WERE EATEN BY A BURNING JEALOUSY...

LOOK HOW HE ENJOYS THE APPLAUSE! IT SHOULD BE OURS... NOT HIS!

QUIET, STUPID! HE COMES!

AH, MON ENFANTS! ANOTHER GOOD SHOW! THE AUDIENCE LIKED KOKO'S ESCAPADES TODAY, AND OUR PURSES ARE FILLED BECAUSE OF OF HIM. SO CLEAN HIM WELL!

WE SHALL SIR, DON'T WORRY! NOW, WHY DON'T YOU GET SOME SLEEP? YOU LOOK TIRED.

BUT IN THE WORKSHOP, WHEN GRAVON HAD GONE TO BED...

BAH! WE THREE DO ALL THE WORK, BUT WE BOW AND SCRAPE TO HIM...

MAYBE WE WON'T ANY LONGER!

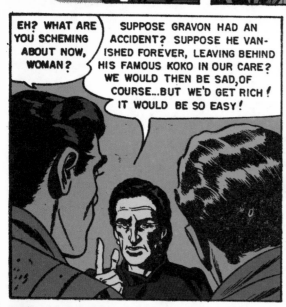

EH? WHAT ARE YOU SCHEMING ABOUT NOW, WOMAN?

SUPPOSE GRAVON HAD AN ACCIDENT? SUPPOSE HE VANISHED FOREVER, LEAVING BEHIND HIS FAMOUS KOKO IN OUR CARE? WE WOULD THEN BE SAD, OF COURSE...BUT WE'D GET RICH! IT WOULD BE SO EASY!

AT FIRST, THE IDEA WAS REPUGNANT TO THE TWO MEN, BUT MARION COAXED, BULLIED AND WHEEDLED. NOW THEY STOOD OUTSIDE GRAVON'S DOOR, DETERMINED, BUT STILL FRIGHTENED...

B...BUT, SUPPOSE HE WAKES UP?

THEN YOU MUST DO IT QUICKLY! NOW, ENTER!

GEORGE, THE WEAKLING, WAS TO BE GRAVON'S NEMESIS! THE DOOR SQEAKED OPEN...A FIGURE STIRRED SLEEPILY IN BED...

WHO...WHO IS IT? ANSWER ME!

NO, NO! AAAARRRRGH

2

IT WAS DONE! SILENTLY THE TRIO CARRIED THE OLD MAN INTO A CRYPT UNDER THE HOUSE! NOW THEY WOULD BURY HIM TO DESTROY HIM FOREVER...

PUT HIM IN THAT OLD COFFIN!

MARION, HE'S MOVING! HE'S ALIVE! AIIIIEEE!

SO *YOU* HAVE DONE THIS TO ME! I...COULD NOT DIE...UNTIL I FOUND OUT! BUT YOU WILL NOT ESCAPE ME... I SHALL...COME BACK... THIS BE MY CURSE ON YOU! *I SHALL...COME... BACK!*

THE KNIFE... GIVE ME THAT KNIFE!

DIE, OLD MAN! DIE, DIE! WE HAVE A RIGHT TO BE RICH! NO ONE WILL EVER FIND YOU...SO YOU CAN CURSE US A HUNDRED TIMES! *WE LAUGH!*

HE CAME BACK FROM THE DEAD! I KNEW WE SHOULDN'T HAVE DONE IT! I WAS A FOOL... A FOOL!

SHUT UP, BLUNDERER! IF YOU HAD DONE YOUR WORK HE'D HAVE BEEN DEAD LONG AGO! NOW, *DIG!* KOKO IS OURS-- AT LAST!

AND, INDEED HE WAS! THE POLICE FOUND NO TRACE OF OLD MAN GRAVON. HIS ASSISTANTS WEPT, THEY REFUSED TO WORK; BUT THE PUBLIC INSISTED, SO THEY PROSPERED...AND BECAME FAMOUS...

THANK YOU... THANK YOU, AND KOKO THANKS YOU, TOO!

BRAVO, KOKO, BRAVO!

CLAP CLAP CLAP

AFTER THE SHOW THEY WOULD WALK HOME AT NIGHT...GLOATING, CONTENTED...COUNTING THEIR MONEY... DREAMING BIG THOUGHTS...

HA, HA, THREE HUNDRED CENTAVOS! NOT BAD!

JUST ANOTHER YEAR OF THIS... AND WE'LL RETIRE! KOKO, MY SWEET... KOKO, MY TREASURE...YOU HAVE DONE THIS!

3

SUDDENLY, FROM OUT OF THE SHADOWS, STEPPED AN EERIE FIGURE...

WHA...?

HEE, HEE...DON'T BE FRIGHTENED, LITTLE MAN! I CAME TO WARN YOU...ALL THREE OF YOU...TO GIVE UP KOKO...BEWARE OF HIM! BEWARE...FOR I KNOW!

WAIT, COME BACK! NOW, WHAT?

OH, LET HER GO! SHE'S JUST A HARMLESS OLD CRONE! BEWARE OF KOKO? HOW SILLY! COME ON...IT'S LATE!

BUT GEORGE COULD NOT FORGET THOSE WORDS, AND AS THE DAYS PASSED BY, HE SAW ON THE PUPPET'S FACE AN ALMOST UNNOTICEABLE CHANGE.

HE'S NOT SMILING ANY MORE...HE'S LEERING...LEERING AT ME!

PSST...IT'S YOUR CUE, GEORGE!

I CAN'T GO ON! GIVE ME ANOTHER PUPPET! I DON'T WANT KOKO! LOOK AT HIS FACE...HE KNOWS! *HE KNOWS!*

GET HOLD OF YOURSELF, FOOL! YOU'LL GIVE US AWAY! I DON'T SEE ANYTHING DIFFERENT! NOW, HURRY UP!

BUT, THAT NIGHT GEORGE SLIPPED INTO THE WORKSHOP TO SEE FOR HIMSELF...

I SWEAR I SAW KOKO MOVE TODAY...AND THAT FACE...IT WAS WATCHING ME ALL DURING THE ACT! ULP! THESE FINGERS... *TH..THEY'RE WEBBED!*

AS THE STUNNED PUPPETEER FELL BACK, THE SMALL HEAD RAISED ITSELF AND LOOKED AT HIM, SMILING EVILLY...

YOU ARE THE FIRST, GEORGE ...ONLY *THE FIRST!*

NO! *STAY BACK!*

HA, HA, HA, HA, HA...

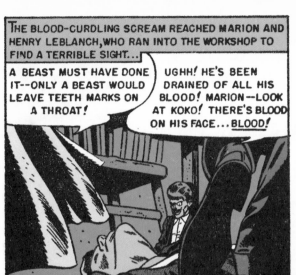

THE BLOOD-CURDLING SCREAM REACHED MARION AND HENRY LEBLANCH, WHO RAN INTO THE WORKSHOP TO FIND A TERRIBLE SIGHT...

A BEAST MUST HAVE DONE IT--ONLY A BEAST WOULD LEAVE TEETH MARKS ON A THROAT!

UGHH! HE'S BEEN DRAINED OF ALL HIS BLOOD! MARION--LOOK AT KOKO! THERE'S BLOOD ON HIS FACE...BLOOD!

LOOK, I TELL YOU! GEORGE WAS RIGHT! THE PUPPET HAS CHANGED... IT'S VICIOUS... GRAVON SAID HE'D COME BACK!

NO...IT CAN'T BE... IT JUST CAN'T BE!

STOP IT! GEORGE MUST HAVE FALLEN AGAINST THE TABLE TO DEFEND HIMSELF FROM WHAT-EVER, WAS ATTACKING HIM! THE PUPPET FELL INTO THIS RED PAINT... SEE? IT'S PAINT... AND NOTHING ELSE!

THE AUTHORITIES COMBED THE COUNTRY SIDE... AND FOUND NOTHING! MARION AND HENRY CON-TINUED TO WORK. AS FOR KOKO, HE WAS MORE AGILE, MORE ACTIVE...JUMPING AS IF HE HAD RENEWED STRENGTH...

WHAT'S WRONG WITH YOU TONIGHT? KOKO ALMOST SLIPPED OUT OF YOUR HANDS!

IT'S UNCANNY! THE STRINGS CAN'T HOLD HIM BACK... I...I ALMOST THINK HE'S ALIVE!

THEN, ONE NIGHT MARION HAD GONE TO THE CITY TO SHOP... HENRY WAS IRRITABLE THAT HIS WIFE WAS NOT WITH HIM...UNEASY WITH AN UNKNOWN DREAD...

I CAN'T READ ANYMORE... WHERE IS SHE? SHE'S LATE!

AH, THERE SHE IS! MARION, WHAT KEPT YOU? I ALMOST STARVED WAITING FOR YOU! I'VE GOT DINNER REA---

GASP...I'M HAVING A NIGHTMARE! IT CAN'T BE REAL!

I HAVE WAITED FOR YOU, HENRY! YOUR TIME HAS COME! HA, HA...

5

P-PLEASE--I..I DON'T WANT TO DIE! I'VE DONE NOTHING! N-NO--Y-A-A-AH!

THE CURSE IS ALMOST FULFILLED! THERE REMAINS--ONE MORE! HA, HA...

A FEW MOMENTS LATER, MARION LEBLANCH ENTERED THE HOUSE, EXCITED FROM HER TRIP TO THE CITY. THEN--SHE SAW IT!

HIS FACE IS PALE-WHITE--LIKE GEORGE'S WAS--DRAINED OF ALL HIS BLOOD! ONLY A VAMPIRE COULD DO THAT--WAIT! THERE'S A BIT OF CLOTH NEARBY--IT'S BEEN TORN!

BLOOD-DROPS--THEY GO DOWN THE BACK STEPS--INTO THE CRYPT! KOKO'S DRESS COAT WAS MADE OUT OF THIS CLOTH! NO--IT'S FANTASTIC--GRAVON'S CURSE CAN'T BE REAL! BUT I'LL FIX HIM AGAIN--TO MAKE SURE!

THE HALF-CRAZED WOMAN, STOPPING ONLY LONG ENOUGH TO PHONE THE POLICE, STAGGERED DOWN THE STEPS INTO THE EERIE TOMB, OBSESSED BUT WITH A SINGLE THOUGHT... I'LL POUND THIS STAKE INTO YOUR ROTTED HEART! ARE YOU LISTENING, GRAVON?

FOR TWENTY MINUTES SHE DUG TO UNEARTH THE COFFIN...MEANWHILE, UPSTAIRS, THE LOCAL CONSTABULARY HAD ARRIVED...

THERE'S THE BODY! WHERE IS MADAME LEBLANCH--AND WHERE'S HER "VAMPIRE"?

WHAT RUBBISH! THE WOMAN'S DAFT! SHE'S THE ONE WHO KILLED BOTH HER BROTHER AND HER HUSBAND! FIND HER AND WE FIND THE MURDERER!

A SCREAM--IT CAME FROM SOMEWHERE IN THE DEPTHS OF THIS HOUSE!

SIR--THERE'S A SMALL PASSAGEWAY LEADING DOWN INTO A VAULT OF SOME KIND! LET'S MAKE HASTE!

IN THE CRYPT, MARION LEBLANCH HAD UNCOVERED THE COFFIN OF JACQUES GRAVON. AND SITTING UP, GORGED WITH BLOOD, WAS A CREATURE FROM THE DEAD--THE VAMPIRE PUPPET!!

YOU ARE IMPATIENT, MY DEAR!

Y-YOU'RE KOKO! B-BUT HOW? THIS IS IMPOSSIBLE! WHERE IS GRAVON?

6

I AM GRAVON! KOKO AND I ARE ONE! HE LIVES THROUGH THE BLOOD OF MORTALS AND I LIVE THROUGH HIM! HA, HA...

GET BACK!

ONE TINY BITE AND IT WILL BE ALL OVER!

NEVER! YOU'LL DIE FIRST...

THE STAKE PLUNGED THROUGH THE VAMPIRE'S HEART AND PUSHED IT BACK INTO THE COFFIN. BUT NOT BEFORE A DYING CLAW HAD TORN THE JUGULAR VEIN FROM ITS VICTIM'S THROAT!

IT'S DRAGGING ME TOWARDS THE COFFIN... IT'S GETTING DARK... COUGH...COUGH...OHH-H...

MOMENTS LATER...

WHAT IS THIS PLACE?

IT'S A BURIAL CRYPT! LOOK... THERE'S A COFFIN OVER THERE... SACRE BLEU...!

IS SHE...?

YES...! BUT THERE'S SOMETHING ELSE PARTLY HIDDEN BY HER BODY...

HA, HA, HA, HA, HA...

THE TWO MEN STOOD THERE...THEY COULD SENSE THE PRESENCE OF THE SUPERNATURAL. AND BACK IN THE SHADOWS, AN OLD CRONE WAS LAUGHING TO HERSELF. ONLY SHE KNEW THAT JACQUES GRAVON'S CURSE HAD BEEN FULFILLED...FOR SHE WAS... DEATH!!!

-THE END-

7

THE DEVIL'S STONES

It happened in 1682, on a farm in New Hampshire. George Walton, a farmer, quarreled with his neighbor over a piece of land...

THIS LAND IS RIGHTLY MINE, I TELL YOU-- AND I MEAN TO HAVE IT!

TAKE IT THEN! BUT YOU SHALL NEVER QUIETLY ENJOY THAT GROUND! YOU HEAR ME? YOU SHALL NEVER QUIETLY ENJOY THAT GROUND!

5-1079

WALTON PAID NO ATTENTION TO THE THREAT. THEN, ON A SUNDAY SOON AFTER...

STONES--INSIDE THE HOUSE! WHERE ARE THEY COMING FROM?

CRASH!

FROM THAT TIME ON, WALTON WAS PLAGUED WITH STONES, EVEN WHEN HE WORKED IN THE FIELDS!

OH! MY HEAD!

HIS MEN KEPT SEARCHING THE GROUNDS, BUT...

THERE'S NO ONE AROUND, MR. WALTON! THOSE ARE THE DEVIL'S STONES!

WALTON FINALLY COMPLAINED TO THE GOVERNOR OF NEW HAMPSHIRE... AND THEN THE SHOWERS OF STONES STOPPED.

IT'S THE DEVIL'S WORK, SIR! MY NEIGHBOR MUST BE A WITCH!

BUT MAN, YOU HAVE NO PROOF!

WALTON NEVER SAW THE STONES AGAIN. BUT THEY WERE NEVER EXPLAINED, AND HE FEARED THEM THE REST OF HIS LIFE...

END

Like the soul-shattering howl of a doomed soul on its way to Hades, came the sound Joe Brixton would never forget! Not even the shriek of a banshee or the screech of a werewolf could compare with this one hideous...

SCREAM IN THE NIGHT

B-1782

Joe Brixton's favorite amusement as he tore along the desert highway on his truck haul was to crush any animals that skittered in his path...

NUMBER 873 COMIN' UP!

THE DUMB MUTT! LOOK AT HIM BLINKIN' AT ME!

TAKE A GOOD LOOK, YOU VARMINT! YOUR LAST ONE!

EEEE!

WH-WHAT IN HECK WAS *THAT?*

A COYOTE! I NEVER MISS, EDDIE! I GOT EIGHT WHEELS ON THIS CRATE--IF I DON'T HIT 'EM WITH ONE, I DO WITH THE OTHER!

YOU'RE A CRUEL SON-OF-A-GUN, JOE! YOU KILL FOR THE FUN OF IT!

IT AIN'T KILLIN' WHEN YOU KILL ANIMALS! THEY'RE BETTER OFF DEAD! THEY WERE BORN TO BE KILLED!

SO ARE YOU! SO'S EVERYBODY! EVERYTHING THAT LIVES, DIES SOMEDAY! BUT DYIN' IS DIFFERENT FROM KILLIN'! DON'T SHOW ME YOUR SCORE SHEETS!

AW, YOU'RE SOFT IN THE HEAD, EDDIE!

I JUST HUNT FOR ANIMALS FOR SPORT! AN' I USE MY TRUCK INSTEAD OF A SHOTGUN!

SPORT, NUTS! IT'S *MURDER!*

NAW! IT'S PASSIN' TIME! YOU GET BORED JUST WATCHIN' THE ROAD! KILLIN' ANIMALS GIVES YOU SOMETHIN' TO DO! AN' I ALWAYS *DID* HATE ANIMALS...

I USED TO ENJOY PULLIN' WINGS OFF BUTTERFLIES... DROWN CATS IN THE RIVER... EVEN STONED A DOG TO DEATH ONCE...

SHUT UP! YOU TURN MY STOMACH!

HA! HA! GOT YOUR GOAT, EH? OKAY, SOFTY! GO BACK TO DREAMLAND... I'M GOIN' AFTER KILL NUMBER 874!

2.

SO EDDIE LOGAN DROPPED OFF TO SLEEP AGAIN, WHILE JOE BRIXTON...

I WONDER WHAT'LL TURN UP NEXT? A RABBIT? A GOPHER! MAYBE A 'STRAY CALF... IT'LL BE GOOD TO KNOCK OFF SOMETHIN' *BIG* FOR A CHANGE...

GUYS LIKE EDDIE... THEY'VE GOT THIN SKINS AN' NO STOMACH... ALWAYS SORRY FOR SOMEBODY... EVEN A COCKROACH...

EDDIE NEVER HEARD THAT THE WEAK CROAK AN' THE STRONG SURVIVE! THAT'S LIFE AN' I'M A STRONG GUY!

...HEY! I THINK I SEE NUMBER 874 COMING UP!

YEAH! THERE SHE IS... BLINDED BY THE HEADLIGHTS! DON'T KNOW WHERE TO RUN! HA-HA! STAND STILL, KITTY... UNCLE JOE WILL BE RIGHT WITH YOU!

IIIIEEE!

AH! SHE SEES IT COMIN' NOW! HA-HA! TOO LATE, KITTY! YOU'RE A HEAP OF NOTHIN'!

NUMBER 874!

WH-WHAT'S THAT?

III-EEEE!

3

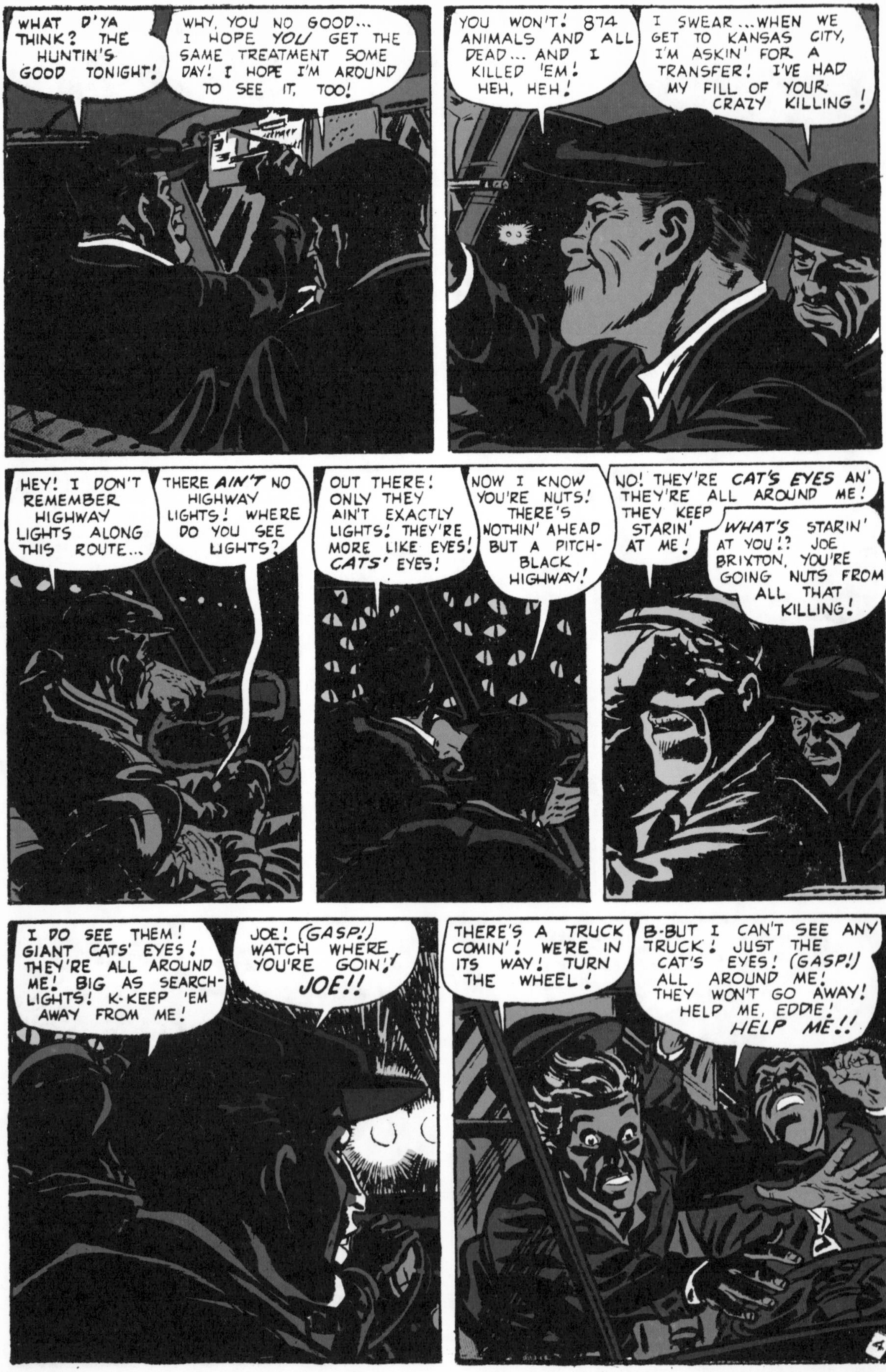
WHAT D'YA THINK? THE HUNTIN'S GOOD TONIGHT!
WHY, YOU NO GOOD... I HOPE YOU GET THE SAME TREATMENT SOME DAY! I HOPE I'M AROUND TO SEE IT, TOO!
YOU WON'T! 874 ANIMALS AND ALL DEAD... AND I KILLED 'EM! HEH, HEH!
I SWEAR...WHEN WE GET TO KANSAS CITY, I'M ASKIN' FOR A TRANSFER! I'VE HAD MY FILL OF YOUR CRAZY KILLING!
HEY! I DON'T REMEMBER HIGHWAY LIGHTS ALONG THIS ROUTE...
THERE AIN'T NO HIGHWAY LIGHTS! WHERE DO YOU SEE LIGHTS?
OUT THERE! ONLY THEY AIN'T EXACTLY LIGHTS! THEY'RE MORE LIKE EYES! CATS' EYES!
NOW I KNOW YOU'RE NUTS! THERE'S NOTHIN' AHEAD BUT A PITCH-BLACK HIGHWAY!
NO! THEY'RE CAT'S EYES AN' THEY'RE ALL AROUND ME! THEY KEEP STARIN' AT ME!
WHAT'S STARIN' AT YOU!? JOE BRIXTON, YOU'RE GOING NUTS FROM ALL THAT KILLING!
I DO SEE THEM! GIANT CATS' EYES! THEY'RE ALL AROUND ME! BIG AS SEARCH-LIGHTS! K-KEEP 'EM AWAY FROM ME!
JOE! (GASP!) WATCH WHERE YOU'RE GOIN'! JOE!!
THERE'S A TRUCK COMIN'! WE'RE IN ITS WAY! TURN THE WHEEL!
B-BUT I CAN'T SEE ANY TRUCK! JUST THE CAT'S EYES! (GASP!) ALL AROUND ME! THEY WON'T GO AWAY! HELP ME, EDDIE! HELP ME!!
4

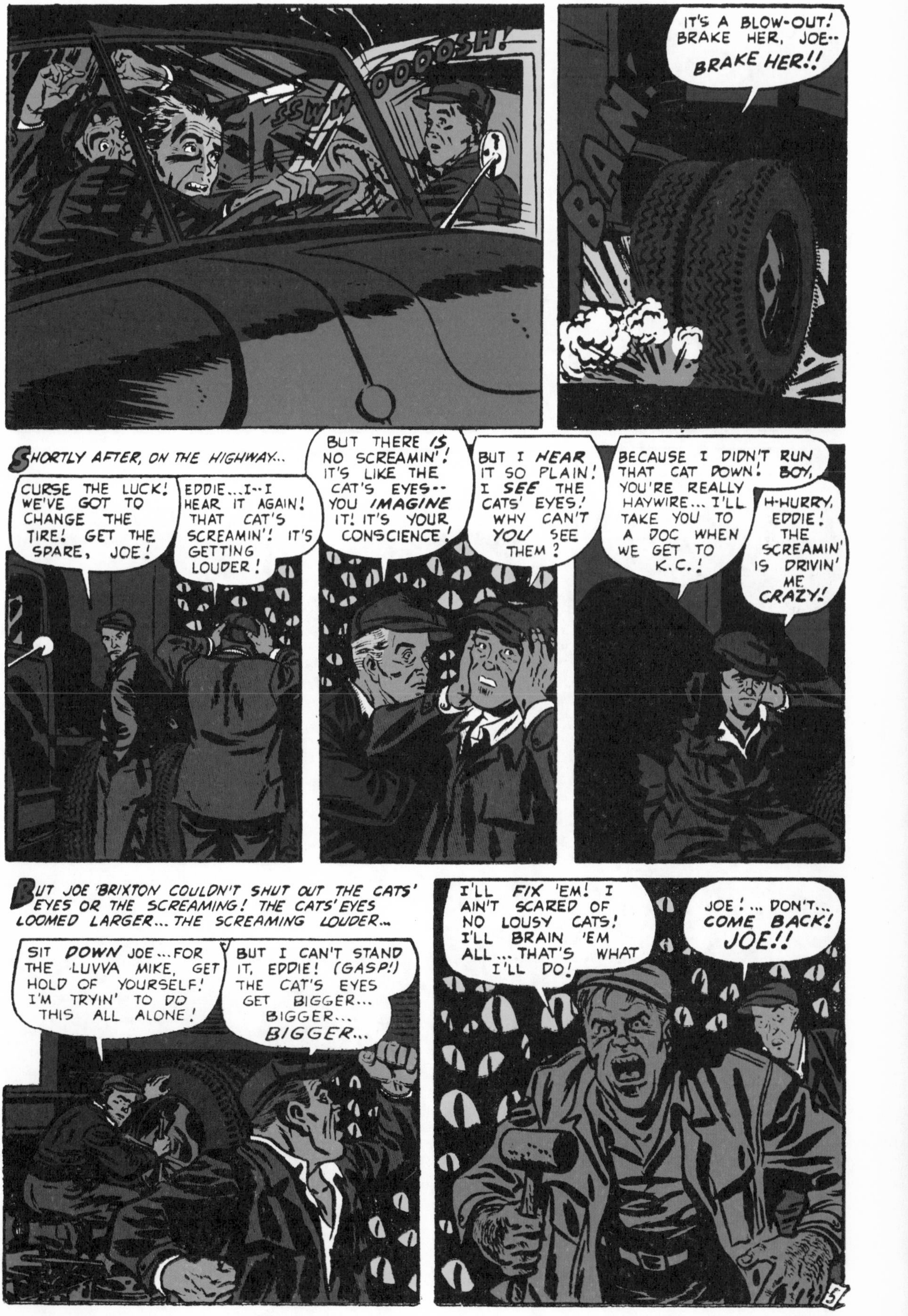
SSWWOOOOOSH!
IT'S A BLOW-OUT! BRAKE HER, JOE-- BRAKE HER!!
BAM!
SHORTLY AFTER, ON THE HIGHWAY...
CURSE THE LUCK! WE'VE GOT TO CHANGE THE TIRE! GET THE SPARE, JOE!
EDDIE... I-- I HEAR IT AGAIN! THAT CAT'S SCREAMIN'! IT'S GETTING LOUDER!
BUT THERE IS NO SCREAMIN'! IT'S LIKE THE CAT'S EYES-- YOU IMAGINE IT! IT'S YOUR CONSCIENCE!
BUT I HEAR IT SO PLAIN! I SEE THE CATS' EYES! WHY CAN'T YOU SEE THEM?
BECAUSE I DIDN'T RUN THAT CAT DOWN! BOY, YOU'RE REALLY HAYWIRE... I'LL TAKE YOU TO A DOC WHEN WE GET TO K.C.!
H-HURRY, EDDIE! THE SCREAMIN' IS DRIVIN' ME CRAZY!
BUT JOE BRIXTON COULDN'T SHUT OUT THE CATS' EYES OR THE SCREAMING! THE CATS' EYES LOOMED LARGER... THE SCREAMING LOUDER...
SIT DOWN JOE... FOR THE LUVVA MIKE, GET HOLD OF YOURSELF! I'M TRYIN' TO DO THIS ALL ALONE!
BUT I CAN'T STAND IT, EDDIE! (GASP!) THE CAT'S EYES GET BIGGER... BIGGER... BIGGER...
I'LL FIX 'EM! I AIN'T SCARED OF NO LOUSY CATS! I'LL BRAIN 'EM ALL... THAT'S WHAT I'LL DO!
JOE! ... DON'T... COME BACK! JOE!!
5

WHATEVER JOE SAW...WHATEVER HE HEARD...JOE WILL NEVER SEE OR HEAR AGAIN... NOT THIS SIDE OF THE GRAVE! The END

The VENGEANCE VAT

IN HER SCABROUS OLD SHACK ON THE EDGE OF A SMOKING, STENCH RIDDEN GARBAGE DUMP, A REPULSIVE OLD CRONE CALLED MYRA SPENT HOURS MUMBLING AND MUTTERING WEIRD INCANTATIONS OVER A VAT OF EVIL-SMELLING BREW! LEFT ALONE, SHE BOTHERED NO ONE. BUT THE DAY THEY TRIED TO EVICT HER, OLD MYRA SUMMONED STRANGE POWERS FROM BEYOND THE GRAVE TO STRIKE BACK AT HER PERSECUTORS IN FRIGHTFUL AND AWESOME WAYS..

YOU SILLY HUMANS THOUGHT YOU COULD DESTROY OLD MYRA! HEH-HEH-HEH! WELL, NOW YOU WILL PAY FOR YOUR MEDDLING WITH A MISTRESS OF THE BLACK ARTS!

I'M FED UP WITH DOING MY BROTHER LARS' DIRTY WORK! NOW, ON TOP OF EVERYTHING ELSE, I'VE GOT TO BE THE ONE TO TELL POOR OLD MYRA SHE'S GOT TO LEAVE, THAT WE'RE TEARING HER SHACK DOWN!

B 1586

WELCOME, ZANE KASLOW!

PHEW! WHAT KIND OF EVIL STUFF ARE YOU BREWING IN THAT UGLY OLD POT, MYRA? THE STEAM SEEMS TO BE FORMING EVIL FACES!

MERELY SOME OF THE EVIL SPIRITS EMBROILED IN MY MAGIC BREW! DON'T BE AFRAID! THEY'LL NOT BOTHER ANYONE WHO LEAVES ME ALONE

MYRA, I'VE BAD NEWS! MY BROTHER, LARS, INSISTS THAT YOU MOVE OUT OF THIS SHACK ON THE EDGE OF THE GARBAGE DUMP! TODAY!

DRAT YOUR WICKED, CONCEITED BROTHER! HOW DARE HE TRY TO ORDER ME AROUND! GO BACK AND TELL HIM THAT ALL THE FORCES OF HADES WILL BE TURNED AGAINST HIM IF HE PERSISTS! HE WILL SUFFER IMMORTAL AGONY!

I KNEW I'D HAVE TO COME DOWN HERE AND DO THE JOB MYSELF! YOU'RE STANDING HERE LISTENING TO THAT CRAZY WITCH-WOMAN TALK, INSTEAD OF GETTING HER OUT OF HERE, ZANE! WHAT'S THE MATTER WITH YOU?

GET OUT! LEAVE ME ALONE!

DON'T TOUCH ME! MY MAGIC BREW WILL BRING SUDDEN DEATH IF YOU TRY TO FORCE ME!

SHUT UP! AND GET OUT!

YOU SHOVED HER TOO HARD, LARS! THAT BLOW SOUNDED AS THOUGH IT CRACKED HER SKULL!

SHE SHE'S DEAD! ZANE, YOU SAW HOW IT HAPPENED. IT WAS AN ACCIDENT! YOU CAN TESTIFY THAT I DIDN'T MEAN TO KILL HER!

COULD I? I COULD ALSO MAKE IT LOOK VERY BAD FOR YOU, LARS, MY HANDSOME, BOSSY BROTHER, UNLESS THERE ARE SOME CHANGES IN OUR BUSINESS!

CHANGES? SURE, ZANE, ANYTHING - IF YOU'LL HELP ME OUT OF THIS JAM! YOU CAN BE THE BOSS OF THE COMPANY FROM NOW ON, JUST LIKE YOU'VE ALWAYS WANTED! I'LL DRIVE A TRUCK, WORK IN THE DUMPS!

THAT'S MORE LIKE IT! OKAY! WE'LL GET RID OF THE CORPSE!

WE'LL JUST BURN THE SHACK DOWN— AND TELL THE POLICE THAT OLD MYRA DIED IN THE FIRE.

OF COURSE! IF I HADN'T GOTTEN SO PANICKY I'D HAVE THOUGHT OF THAT TOO!

THERE'LL BE NOTHING BUT ASHES IN A FEW MIN---

FOOLS! YOU THINK TO GET RID OF MYRA SO EASILY? ZANE, BECAUSE YOU HAVE CONSPIRED WITH LARS TO COVER UP MY DEATH, YOU SHALL SUFFER WITH HIM! WITH MY VENGEANCE BREW I'LL PUNISH YOU BOTH!

AYIIE! LOOK, ZANE!

WE DIDN'T REALLY SEE MYRA OF COURSE! IT WAS OUR IMAGINATIONS!

OR SOME KIND OF CRAZY OPTICAL ILLUSION! BUT IT SCARED ME STIFF FOR A FEW MINUTES!

LATER...

BUT, LARS, YOU PROMISED THINGS WERE GOING TO CHANGE IF I HELPED YOU TO—

HA-HA! WELL I'VE CHANGED MY MIND AGAIN! NOW FORGET THAT SILLY TALK ABOUT YOUR BEING BOSS AND GET BACK UP ON THE TRUCK!

DON'T FORGET, NOW THAT THE POLICE HAVE DECLARED MYRA'S DEATH ACCIDENTAL, YOU'RE AS GUILTY AS I AM, FOR HELPING COVER UP THE CRIME! SO YOU HAVE NO HOLD ON ME!

THE DIRTY DOUBLE-CROSSER! I'LL FIX HIM!

THE NEXT DAY..

HOLD IT A MINUTE, ZANE! THIS LOOKS LIKE A USABLE PIECE OF MACHINERY! GOOD THING I SPOTTED IT BEFORE YOU BURIED IT UNDER THAT LOAD OF SCRAP IRON.

THIS IS MY CHANCE!

KASLOW GARBAGE COLLECTOR

ZANE, WAIT! TURN OFF THE DUMPING MECHANISM!

WHAT FOR? NOW I'LL HAVE THE WHOLE BUSINESS TO MYSELF! LET'S SEE YOU TALK YOUR WAY OUT OF THIS, SMART GUY!

I MUST NOT BE FRIGHTENED! NOBODY CAN PROVE IT WASN'T AN ACCIDENT! NOW TO GO TO THE POLICE AND BLUFF THE THING THROUGH!

RRRRRRRR

SIX MONTHS LATER..

GETTING RID OF LARS WAS THE SMARTEST THING I EVER DID! BUSINESS IS BETTER THAN EVER SINCE I'VE BEEN RUNNING IT! AND CATHY, LARS' WIDOW, SEEMS EVEN HAPPIER, MARRIED TO ME! THIS IS THE LIFE!

HI, DARLING!

KASLOW GARBAGE DISPOSAL

BUT THAT NIGHT.

BEWARE, ZANE KASLOW! IT IS ALMOST TIME FOR MY VENGEANCE BREW TO TAKE EFFECT ON YOU! BECAUSE YOU ONCE PRETENDED TO BE MY FRIEND, YOU ARE CURSED TO SUFFER AN EVEN WORSE FATE THAN LARS!

GO AWAY!

I TELL YOU SHE WAS HERE! MYRA, THE OLD WITCH! MAY-MAYBE SHE ISN'T REALLY DEAD! I-I'M SCARED!

OH, STOP IT, ZANE! YOU JUST HAD A NIGHTMARE! GO ON BACK TO SLEEP!

FOR SEVERAL WEEKS NOW I'VE BEEN HAVING THOSE HORRIBLE NIGHTMARES! I'M LOSING WEIGHT! SOMETIMES I THINK I'M GOING CRAZY! YET NOTHING SEEMS TO STOP THEM! COULD THAT OLD HAG REALLY HAVE PUT A CURSE ON ME?

THAT NIGHT..

CATHY! THAT-THAT OLD WITCH'S CAULDRON! WHERE DID IT COME FROM? IT'S LIKE OLD MYRA'S! AND THE FUMES ARE FORMING FACES OF EVIL!

I DON'T SEE ANY FACES IN THE STEAM! I BOUGHT THIS FROM AN OLD WOMAN JUNK PEDDLER! YOU KNOW HOW CRAZY I AM ABOUT ANTIQUES!

IT'S THE SAME VAT, I TELL YOU! IT'S COME BACK TO HAUNT ME! YOU'VE GOT TO GET RID OF IT! WHY ARE YOU COOKING THAT MESS IN IT?

JUST EXPERIMENTING WITH A RECIPE I FOUND PRINTED ON THE BOTTOM OF THE POT! I'LL THROW IT OUT-BUT I'M KEEPING THE CAULDRON!

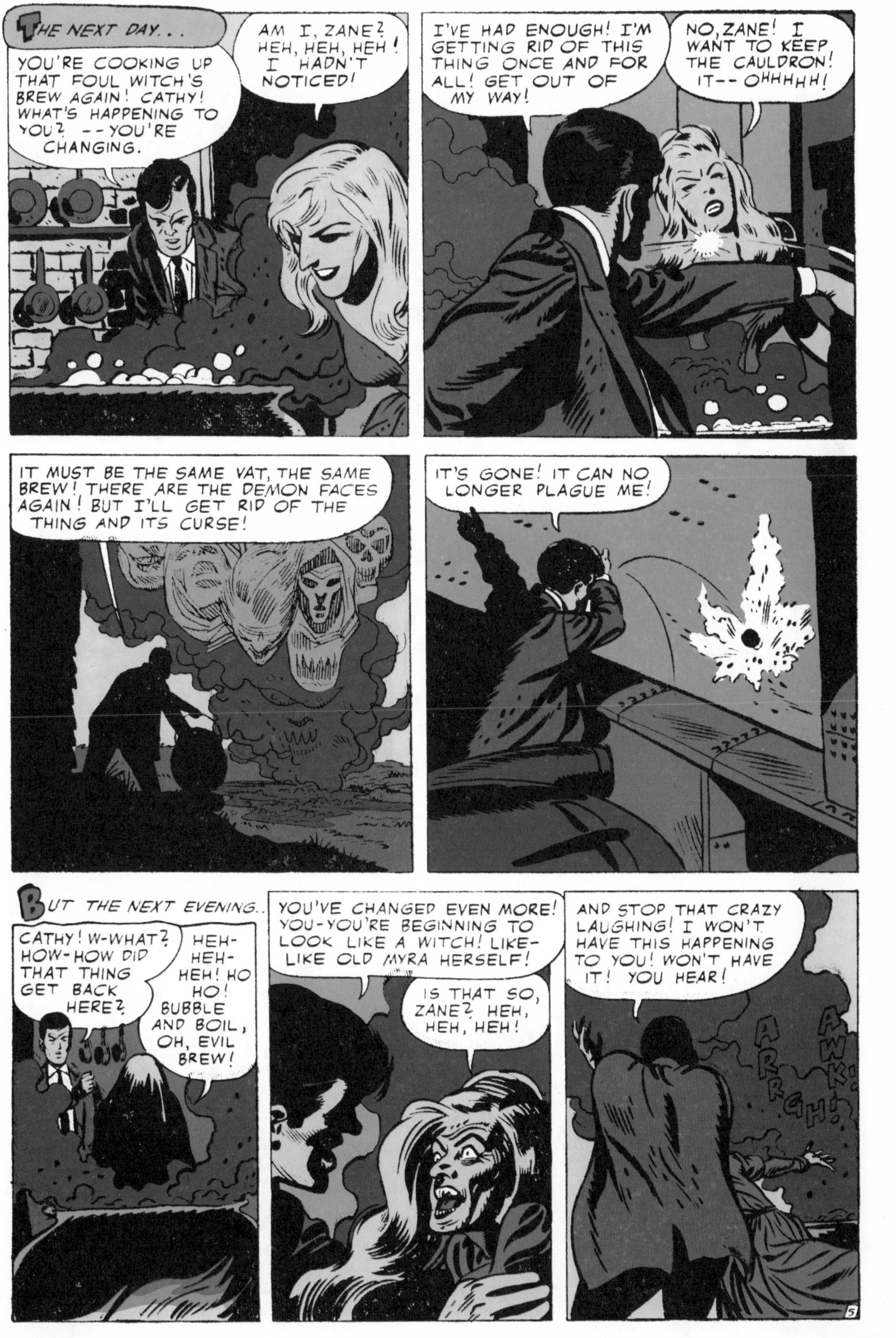
THE NEXT DAY...
YOU'RE COOKING UP THAT FOUL WITCH'S BREW AGAIN! CATHY! WHAT'S HAPPENING TO YOU? --YOU'RE CHANGING.
AM I, ZANE? HEH, HEH, HEH! I HADN'T NOTICED!
I'VE HAD ENOUGH! I'M GETTING RID OF THIS THING ONCE AND FOR ALL! GET OUT OF MY WAY!
NO, ZANE! I WANT TO KEEP THE CAULDRON! IT--OHHHHHH!
IT MUST BE THE SAME VAT, THE SAME BREW! THERE ARE THE DEMON FACES AGAIN! BUT I'LL GET RID OF THE THING AND ITS CURSE!
IT'S GONE! IT CAN NO LONGER PLAGUE ME!
BUT THE NEXT EVENING..
CATHY! W-WHAT? HOW-HOW DID THAT THING GET BACK HERE?
HEH-HEH-HEH! HO HO! BUBBLE AND BOIL, OH, EVIL BREW!
YOU'VE CHANGED EVEN MORE! YOU-YOU'RE BEGINNING TO LOOK LIKE A WITCH! LIKE-LIKE OLD MYRA HERSELF!
IS THAT SO, ZANE? HEH, HEH, HEH!
AND STOP THAT CRAZY LAUGHING! I WON'T HAVE THIS HAPPENING TO YOU! WON'T HAVE IT! YOU HEAR!
ARRGH!
AWK!
5

WAIT! I-I'M SORRY! COME BACK, CATHY! I WON'T HURT YOU ANY MORE! WE'LL FIND SOME WAY TO CHANGE YOU BACK AGAIN, GET RID OF THIS CURSE.

SHE'S GONE! VANISHED INTO THE FOG! BUT SHE'LL COME BACK! I-I'VE GOT TO GET SOME SLEEP.

BUT SLEEP THAT NIGHT WAS ONE TERROR-RIDDEN NIGHTMARE AFTER ANOTHER...

NO! NO! EEIIYEE! HELP! LEAVE ME ALONE.

THE FOLLOWING MORNING...

THAT SHACK! JUST LIKE THE ONE MYRA USED TO LIVE IN! BUT IT CAN'T BE! WE BURNED THE SHACK DOWN!

SOMEBODY MUST BE PLAYING SOME KIND OF WEIRD JOKE ON ME! THE OLD HUT IS EXACTLY LIKE MYRA'S!

MYRA! AND-AND THAT VAT-YOUR VENGEANCE VAT-HERE, NOW! BUT IT CAN'T BE YOU, MYRA! YOU'RE DEAD! DEAD!

AM I ZANE?

YOU'VE COME BACK FROM THE DEAD TO TAUNT ME! BUT THIS TIME I'LL REALLY FINISH YOU!

NO! WAIT ZANE! YOU DON'T KNOW WHAT YOU'RE DOING.

6

THERE! NO ONE COULD LIVE AFTER THAT BATTERING! SHE--WAIT! SOME-SOMETHING'S HAPPENING TO HER! THE CORPSE IS--IS CHANGING INTO--

CATHY! IT MUST HAVE BEEN HER ALL THE TIME, AND MY OVERWROUGHT IMAGINATION MADE HER LOOK LIKE MYRA! OR ELSE I'M GOING MAD!

THE POLICE WILL GET ME FOR THE MURDER OF MY WIFE! GOT TO RUN! KEEP RUNNING FOR EVER AND EVER!

GUILT-TORTURED AND FEARFUL, ZANE KASLOW BECAME A BUM, KEPT ON THE MOVE, BUT HE COULD NEVER COMPLETELY ESCAPE...

THAT SHACK ON THE GARBAGE DUMP! IT'S MILES FROM OUR PLACE, YET THE SHACK LOOKS EXACTLY THE SAME! I-I'VE GOT TO LOOK INSIDE, MAKE SURE!

SURPRISED AT FINDING US HERE, ZANE! DON'T BE! YOU'LL FIND US IN MANY PLACES! HEH-HEH!

AAAIIEE!! CATHY AND MYRA COMBINED INTO ONE FOULLY HIDEOUS BEING!

IN THE MADDENING MONTHS THAT FOLLOWED, WHEREVER HE WENT THERE WAS ALWAYS A GARBAGE DUMP, ALWAYS THE SAME SHACK AND THE SAME HORRIBLE OCCUPANT...

WH-WHAT DO YOU WANT? WH-WH-WHY DON'T YOU LEAVE ME ALONE, YOU CREATURES OF THE DEAD!

WE WILL--WHEN YOU RETURN HOME AND ATONE FOR YOUR CRIMES, ZANE! THAT IS THE ONLY WAY YOU'LL HAVE PEACE.

7

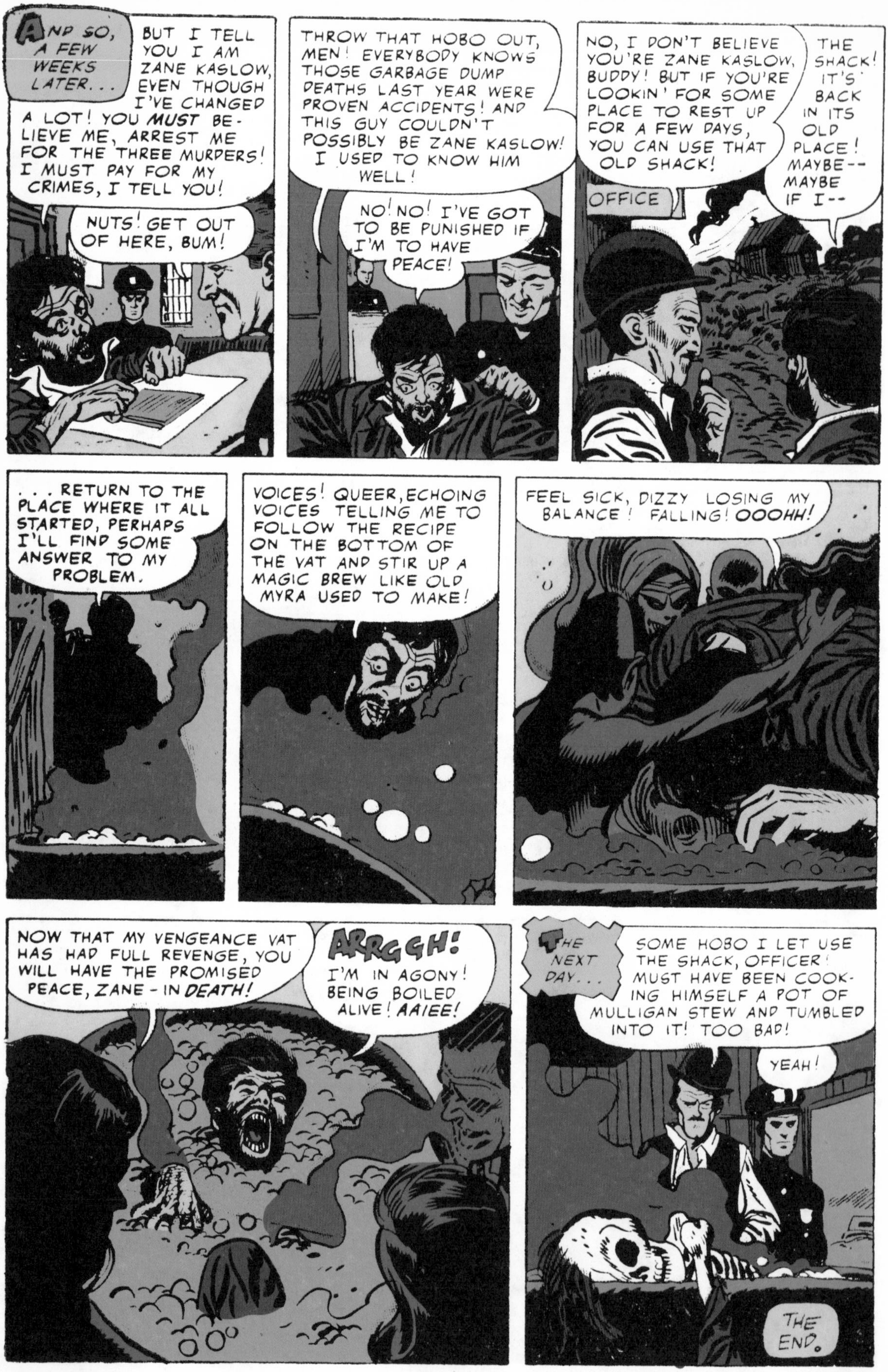
AND SO, A FEW WEEKS LATER...
BUT I TELL YOU I AM ZANE KASLOW, EVEN THOUGH I'VE CHANGED A LOT! YOU MUST BELIEVE ME, ARREST ME FOR THE THREE MURDERS! I MUST PAY FOR MY CRIMES, I TELL YOU!
NUTS! GET OUT OF HERE, BUM!
THROW THAT HOBO OUT, MEN! EVERYBODY KNOWS THOSE GARBAGE DUMP DEATHS LAST YEAR WERE PROVEN ACCIDENTS! AND THIS GUY COULDN'T POSSIBLY BE ZANE KASLOW! I USED TO KNOW HIM WELL!
NO! NO! I'VE GOT TO BE PUNISHED IF I'M TO HAVE PEACE!
NO, I DON'T BELIEVE YOU'RE ZANE KASLOW, BUDDY! BUT IF YOU'RE LOOKIN' FOR SOME PLACE TO REST UP FOR A FEW DAYS, YOU CAN USE THAT OLD SHACK!
OFFICE
THE SHACK! IT'S BACK IN ITS OLD PLACE! MAYBE-- MAYBE IF I--
...RETURN TO THE PLACE WHERE IT ALL STARTED, PERHAPS I'LL FIND SOME ANSWER TO MY PROBLEM.
VOICES! QUEER, ECHOING VOICES TELLING ME TO FOLLOW THE RECIPE ON THE BOTTOM OF THE VAT AND STIR UP A MAGIC BREW LIKE OLD MYRA USED TO MAKE!
FEEL SICK, DIZZY LOSING MY BALANCE! FALLING! OOOHH!
NOW THAT MY VENGEANCE VAT HAS HAD FULL REVENGE, YOU WILL HAVE THE PROMISED PEACE, ZANE - IN DEATH!
ARRGGH!
I'M IN AGONY! BEING BOILED ALIVE! AAIEE!
THE NEXT DAY...
SOME HOBO I LET USE THE SHACK, OFFICER! MUST HAVE BEEN COOKING HIMSELF A POT OF MULLIGAN STEW AND TUMBLED INTO IT! TOO BAD!
YEAH!
THE END.

THE VAMPIRE GOES WEST!

IORIO & TRAPANI

THAR'S OLE SAM MORROW-- WATCHIN' THE STAGE COME IN!

OLDEST AND ORNERIEST SHERIFF IN THUH WEST, SAM IS! BUT YUH GOTTA HAND IT TO HIM THOUGH-- *HE SHORE CLEANED THUH OWLHOOTS OUTTA THIS-HERE TERRITORY!*

THET'S WHY HE'S ALWAYS ON HAND TO GREET THUH STAGE EVERY TIME IT COMES! HE WANTS TO MAKE PLUMB SHORE *THEY NEVER COME BACK!*

HEY, **YOU!** WHUT'S YORE BUSINESS HERE?

YOU ARE ADDRESSING ME, SIR?

MY NAME IS RUDOLF SEVARIAN! I AM HERE FOR MY HEALTH!

HEALTH, HUH? **HMMM--** COULD BE! YUH SHORE LOOK LIVERISH! HOTEL'S ACROSS THUH STREET!

A PRIVATE ROOM, PLEASE! IT MUST HAVE A WINDOW!

SEE YUH INSPECTED THUH NEWCOMER, SAM, JIST LIKE YUH ALWAYS DO!

THET'S MY JOB! NEVER LAY DOWN ON MY JOB!

THAT ELDERLY GENTLEMAN WITH THE OBJECT ENCASED IN LEATHER HANGING FROM THE END OF HIS WATCH CHAIN--WHO IS HE, PLEASE?

HIM? THET'S SAM MORROW--OUR SHERIFF! SAM AIN'T AS YOUNG AS HE USETA BE, BUT HE KIN STILL OUT-DRAW ANY MAN AROUND!

THAT OBJECT HANGING FROM HIS WATCH CHAIN--WHY DOES HE KEEP TWIRLING IT?

THAT? FOLKS AROUND HERE THINK A LOT OF SAM! AFTER HE CLEANED OUT THUH BLACK DEATH GANG NIGH ONTO TWENTY YEARS AGO, EVERYBODY GOT TOGETHER AN' GAVE HIM **THAT** TO HANG ON HIS CHAIN AS A SORT OF TOKEN! SAM SHORE APPRECIATED IT! BEEN WEARIN' IT EVER SINCE! EVEN TAKES IT TO SLEEP WITH HIM, FOLKS SAY...

HOW, AMUSING! THANK YOU SO MUCH FOR THE INFORMATION!

WHUT THUH--?! I'LL HAVE TO DO SUMPTHIN' ABOUT THET MIRROR! THUH TWO OF US ARE STANDIN' HERE, BUT IT'S REFLECTIN' **ONLY ME!**

THE FOOL'S MIRROR IS IN PERFECT ORDER! **MIRRORS NEVER REFLECT VAMPIRES!**

IT WAS PAST MIDNIGHT NOW! AND AS THE OLD SHERIFF SLEPT IN HIS NARROW BED...

THE VAMPIRE SOARED UP INTO THE SKY!

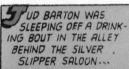

JUD BARTON WAS SLEEPING OFF A DRINKING BOUT IN THE ALLEY BEHIND THE SILVER SLIPPER SALOON...

SUDDENLY...

WH-WHUT'S THAT COMIN' TOWARD ME? AIN'T NEVER SEEN ANYTHIN' LIKE TH-THAT BEFORE!

AND YOU NEVER WILL AGAIN, FOOL! YOU NEVER WILL AGAIN...!

AAARGH!

HOW WISE I WAS TO TRAVEL HERE TO THE AMERICAN WEST! NOBODY HAS EVER EVEN HEARD OF VAMPIRES HERE! BACK HOME IN HUNGARY WE ARE TOO WELL KNOWN! EVERY LAST PEASANT KNOWS THAT IT TAKES ONLY A WOODEN STAKE OR A SILVER BULLET IN OUR HEART TO KILL US! BUT HERE, NOBODY KNOWS... NOBODY KNOWS!

JUST THEN...

WHUT'S GOIN' ON IN THAR! I HEARD A MAN YELLIN'!

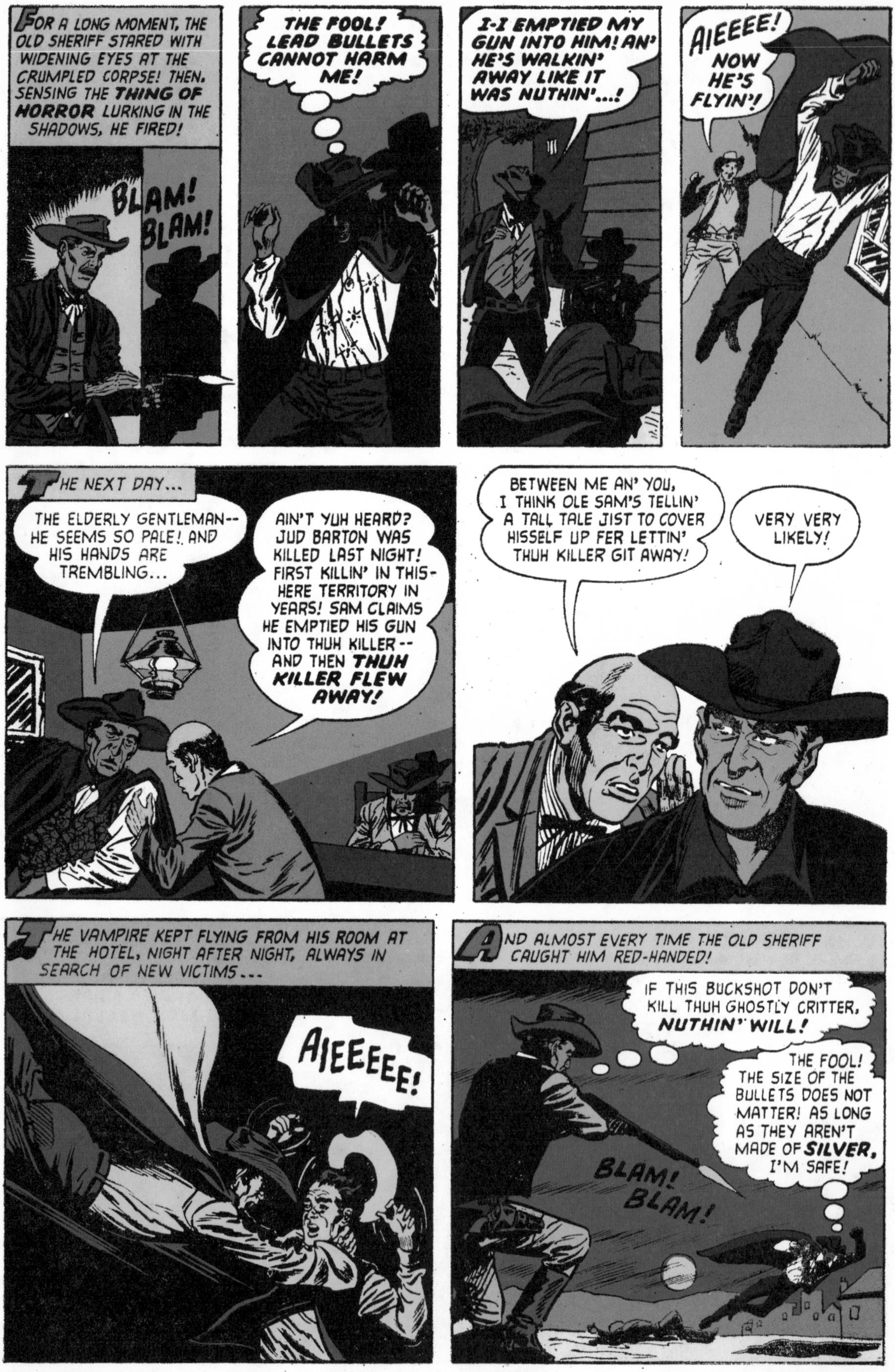
FOR A LONG MOMENT, THE OLD SHERIFF STARED WITH WIDENING EYES AT THE CRUMPLED CORPSE! THEN, SENSING THE THING OF HORROR LURKING IN THE SHADOWS, HE FIRED!
BLAM! BLAM!
THE FOOL! LEAD BULLETS CANNOT HARM ME!
I-I EMPTIED MY GUN INTO HIM! AN' HE'S WALKIN' AWAY LIKE IT WAS NUTHIN'...!
AIEEEE! NOW HE'S FLYIN'!
THE NEXT DAY...
THE ELDERLY GENTLEMAN-- HE SEEMS SO PALE! AND HIS HANDS ARE TREMBLING...
AIN'T YUH HEARD? JUD BARTON WAS KILLED LAST NIGHT! FIRST KILLIN' IN THIS-HERE TERRITORY IN YEARS! SAM CLAIMS HE EMPTIED HIS GUN INTO THUH KILLER-- AND THEN THUH KILLER FLEW AWAY!
BETWEEN ME AN' YOU, I THINK OLE SAM'S TELLIN' A TALL TALE JIST TO COVER HISSELF UP FER LETTIN' THUH KILLER GIT AWAY!
VERY VERY LIKELY!
THE VAMPIRE KEPT FLYING FROM HIS ROOM AT THE HOTEL, NIGHT AFTER NIGHT, ALWAYS IN SEARCH OF NEW VICTIMS...
AIEEEEEE!
AND ALMOST EVERY TIME THE OLD SHERIFF CAUGHT HIM RED-HANDED!
IF THIS BUCKSHOT DON'T KILL THUH GHOSTLY CRITTER, NUTHIN' WILL!
THE FOOL! THE SIZE OF THE BULLETS DOES NOT MATTER! AS LONG AS THEY AREN'T MADE OF SILVER, I'M SAFE!
BLAM! BLAM!

THET'S THE *FIFTH* KILLIN' IN TWO WEEKS!

SAM MORROW'S TOO DURNED OLD TO BE SHERIFF! 'BET THUH KILLER WOULD'VE BEEN TRACKED DOWN LONG AGO IF WE HAD A YOUNGER MAN WEARIN' THET BADGE!

SHHHH-- THAR COMES SAM NOW!

THE ELDERLY GENTLEMAN SEEMS VERY UNHAPPY OF LATE! HE NO LONGER SWINGS THE TOKEN ON THE END OF HIS WATCH CHAIN....

SHORE LOOKS BAD FER SAM! ALL THOSE KILLIN'S HERE LATELY HAVE TURNED FOLKS AGAINST HIM! THEY'RE HOLDIN' A BIG MEETING TONIGHT TO SEE WHUT THEY KIN DO ABOUT *TAKIN' HIS BADGE FROM HIM!*

THAR HE COMES NOW!

HATE TO DO THIS-- 'JIST KNOW HE'LL TAKE IT TO HEART SUMPTHIN' TERRIBLE!

WE AIN'T GOT NO CHOICE -- 'LESS WE WANT TO WAIT TILL *EVERYBODY'S* KILLED!

MEETING HOUSE

NOW EVERYBODY HERE RESPECTS SAM MORROW FER WHUT HE'S DONE FER US IN THUH PAST! BUT...

STOP! WHY DON'T YUH COME RIGHT OUT AN' SAY IT! *I'M NO GOOD ANY MORE!* I KEEP LETTIN' THUH KILLER SLIP THROUGH MY FINGERS! *YUH WANT THUH BADGE --RIGHT? WAL...*

HERE...(SOB)... IT IS!

LET HIM GO! NUTHIN' YUH'D SAY COULD HELP SAM NOW...

THIS SHOULD BE AMUSING! I THINK I'LL FOLLOW THE OLD MAN....

TH-THEY'RE RIGHT! *I'M NO GOOD!* KILLIN' AFTER KILLIN'... *(SOB)*...AN' I CAN'T DO A THING ABOUT IT! *I DON'T DESERVE FOLKS' RESPECT!*

THE SHADOWS ARE THICK HERE -- HE CANNOT SEE ME THROUGH THE WINDOW! *AAAH,* WHAT THE OLD MAN WOULD GIVE TO KNOW WHAT EVERY LAST PEASANT IN HUNGARY KNOWS ABOUT VAMPIRES...!

WH-WHY DO I KEEP THINKIN' OF THET BIG GET-TOGETHER AFTER I DRUV OUT THUH BLACK DEATH GANG? THUH SPEECHES FOLKS MADE...THUH *TOKEN* THEY GAVE ME? *I'M NO GOOD! I NEVER DESERVED THEIR RESPECT!*

HE'S TEARING THE TOKEN FROM THE WATCH CHAIN! HE'S ...

AAAARGH!

I-I DIDN'T DESERVE THUH TOKEN -- I NEVER DESERVED IT! THET'S WHY I ...*(SOB)*...TORE IT FROM THUH CHAIN! THET'S WHY I JAMMED IT INTO MY GUN ...*(SOB)*...AN' FIRED IT THROUGH THUH WINDOW!

IT'S...*(SOB)*...GONE NOW -- MY TOKEN, *MY SILVER BULLET* THET I'VE BEEN CARRYIN' ON MY CHAIN ALL THESE YEARS! *IT'S GONE!*

THE ACCURSED

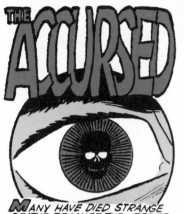

MANY HAVE DIED STRANGE DEATHS BECAUSE THEY DEFIED THE CURSE THAT WAS PUT ON A PARTICULAR OBJECT OR PLACE—FOR BY THEIR DEFIANCE THEY BECAME THE ACCURSED, WHO ALWAYS PAY THE PENALTY FOR FLOUTING THE WISHES OF THE DEAD!

EACH OF THE THREE BRITISH EXPLORERS WHO ENTERED THE TOMB OF THE EGYPTIAN KING, TUTANKHAMEN, DIED UNDER MYSTERIOUS CIRCUMSTANCES...

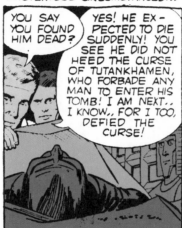

YOU SAY YOU FOUND HIM DEAD?

YES! HE EXPECTED TO DIE SUDDENLY! YOU SEE HE DID NOT HEED THE CURSE OF TUTANKHAMEN, WHO FORBADE ANY MAN TO ENTER HIS TOMB! I AM NEXT.. I KNOW.., FOR I TOO, DEFIED THE CURSE!

STRANGE TOO, WAS THE FATE OF AN ENTIRE COMMUNITY, BACK IN THE '60's, WHEN THEY UNLAWFULLY TOOK SOME LAND FROM THE NEZ PERCE INDIANS...

HEAR MY CURSE, O GREAT SPIRIT! THE CURSE OF WHITE SNOW, NEZ PERCE CHIEFTAIN! LET THE RIVER DRY UP, LET THE CROPS WITHER, LET THE CHILDREN OF THE PALEFACE SICKEN, AND HIS WOMEN DIE FOR THIS TREACHERY!

IT'S WHITE SNOW! I RECKON HE'S LOOKIN' FOR TROUBLE!

WAAL, LET'S GIVE IT TO HIM!

B-1791

THAT'LL TEACH YOU NOT TO COME SNOOPIN' AROUND, INJUN!

YOU WILL PAY, PALEFACE, FOR THE GREAT SPIRIT HAS HEARD MY CURSE, AND... UHHHH...

HE'S DEAD!

WHITE SNOW'S MALEDICTION CAME TO PASS, FOR THE COMMUNITY WAS STRICKEN -- THE WOMEN DIED, THE CROPS FAILED, AND THE CHILDREN SICKENED DURING A SUMMER OF RELENTLESS DROUGHT!

MOST FAMOUS OF ALL CURSES WAS THE ONE PLACED ON THE CRUEL PHARAOH OF EGYPT, IN BIBLICAL TIMES WHEN THE RED SEA CLOSED OVER HIS LEGIONS DROWNING THEM TO THE MAN BECAUSE HE HAD DEFIED THE LORD, AND PURSUED THE FLEEING ISRAELITES!

IN THE SUPERSTITION MOUNTAINS OF ARIZONA, THERE IS A FABULOUS GOLD MINE CALLED THE LOST DUTCHMAN. IT HAS A CURSE ON IT...

YOU SHOT ME IN THE BACK AN' TOOK THE MAP -- BUT IT WON'T DO YUH NO GOOD! NOBODY'LL EVER REACH THE LOST DUTCHMAN AND COME OUT ALIVE!

AHH SHUT UP AN' CROAK! I GOT THE MAP, AN' THAT'S ALL I CARE ABOUT! NOW, I'LL BE RICH!

BUT THE CURSE HAS KEPT EVERYONE FROM THE LOST DUTCHMAN ... THE MAP IS GONE.... AND THE ONLY MAN EVER TO PUT HANDS ON IT WAS KILLED BY THE APACHES WHILE MAKING HIS WAY TO THE MINE! THERE'S A FORTUNE WAITING FOR ANYONE WHO CAN FIND THE LOST DUTCHMAN, THAT IS, IF HE CAN SURVIVE THE CURSE AS WELL!

CARE TO TRY?

The End

GHOST on the GALLOWS

His heart was a rotten apple, and maggots of evil crawled in his brain — but no one knew! He murdered and got away with it! But you can't fool all of the ghosts all of the time, as young Jasper Crandall found out! He also found out another gruesome fact of DEATH — what happens WHEN YOU GIVE A MAN ENOUGH ROPE...

EEEAAAHHHHHHHHHHHH—

Night in New York! The gloomy antique shop of Ferris and Crandall...

WE MIGHT AS WELL FACE IT, JASPER! WE'RE BROKE! AND I'M OLD, SICK AND DISCOURAGED! SOMETIMES I FEEL LIKE KILLING MYSELF!

THAT'S NO WAY TO TALK, MR. FERRIS! WHILE THERE'S LIFE, THERE'S HOPE!

BUT IT'S AN IDEA, AT THAT, YOU OLD FOOL! THERE'S STILL ENOUGH MONEY LEFT—FOR ONE MAN! IF SOMETHING SHOULD HAPPEN TO YOU!

THE DEVIL HELPS THOSE WHO HELP THEMSELVES, SO THE NEXT NIGHT...

AFTER —(CHUCKLE)— THINKING IT OVER, I'VE DECIDED TO HELP OLD FERRIS GET HIS WISH! HE *IS* GOING TO COMMIT SUICIDE!

THIS SHOULD DO IT! AND SINCE HE'S TOLD EVERYONE HIS TROUBLES, IT WILL ONLY LOOK NATURAL WHEN HE — (HAH-HAH) — *HANGS* HIMSELF!

HMMM — WORSE THAN I THOUGHT! WE'RE BANKRUPT! RUINED!

DON'T LET IT WORRY YOU, OLD MAN! *YOUR* TROUBLES WILL ALL BE OVER IN A MINUTE!

AHHRRRGGG— UHHHHHGGG—

SORRY, OLD MAN, BUT SOMETIMES *TWO* IS A CROWD! AND YOU'RE BETTER OFF DEAD ANYWAY!

AFTER THE GRISLY DEED IS DONE...

NOTHING TO IT! THERE SHOULD BE A COUPLE OF THOUSAND IN CASH AND SOME RARE JEWELS THAT OUR CREDITORS DON'T KNOW ABOUT! I —(CHUCKLE)— CAN'T HELP IT IF FERRIS SPENT EVERYTHING BEFORE HE HANGED HIMSELF!

STILL LATER...

I'LL *FIND* THE BODY IN THE MORNING! AFTER THE INQUEST I'LL FILE FOR BANKRUPTCY! THEN I'LL GO AWAY SOMEWHERE AND DISPOSE OF THE JEWELS! MUST BE WORTH AT LEAST TEN THOUSAND! ONLY THING IS — WHERE CAN I GO?

2

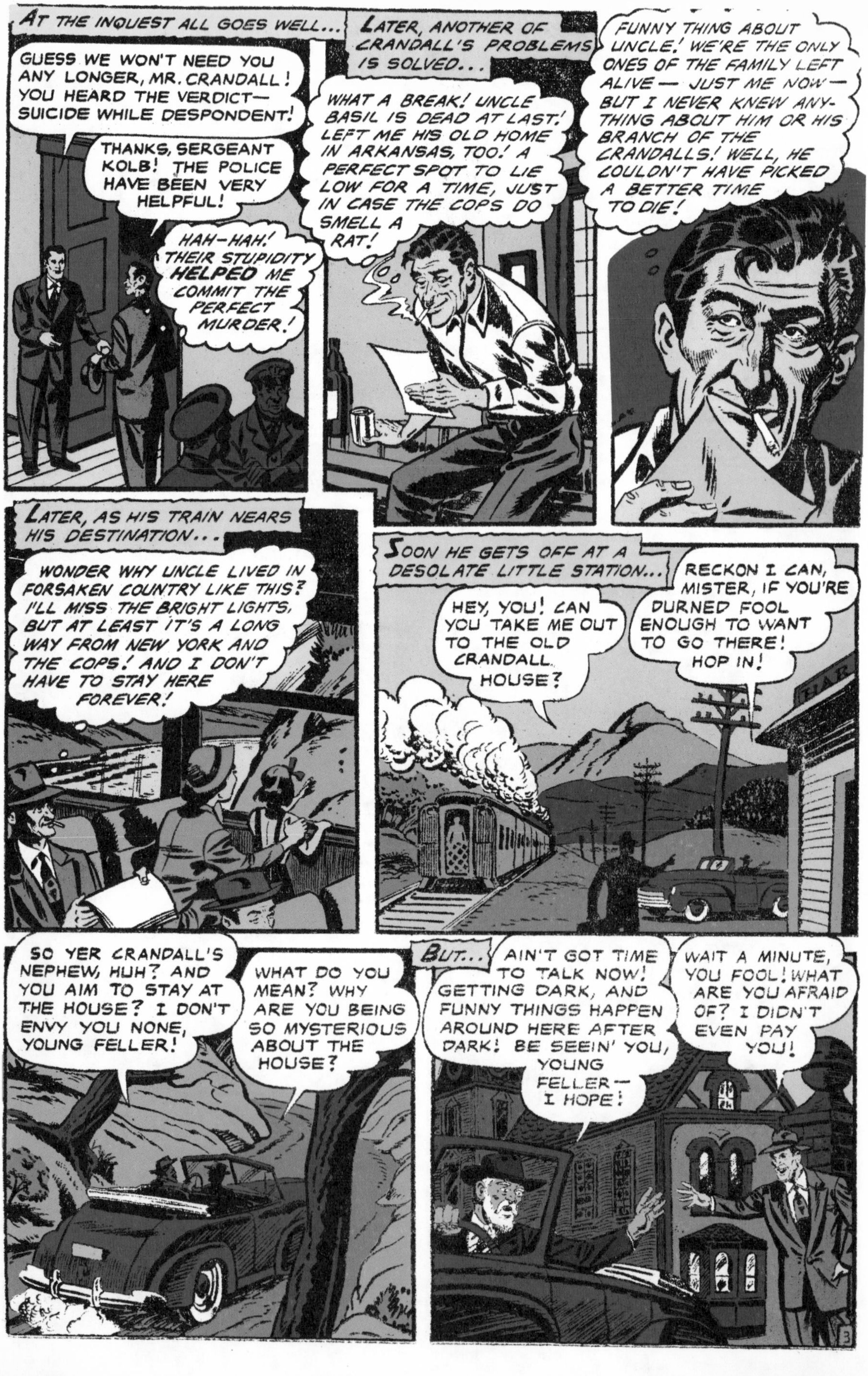
AT THE INQUEST ALL GOES WELL...
GUESS WE WON'T NEED YOU ANY LONGER, MR. CRANDALL! YOU HEARD THE VERDICT— SUICIDE WHILE DESPONDENT!
THANKS, SERGEANT KOLB! THE POLICE HAVE BEEN VERY HELPFUL!
HAH-HAH! THEIR STUPIDITY HELPED ME COMMIT THE PERFECT MURDER!
LATER, ANOTHER OF CRANDALL'S PROBLEMS IS SOLVED...
WHAT A BREAK! UNCLE BASIL IS DEAD AT LAST! LEFT ME HIS OLD HOME IN ARKANSAS, TOO! A PERFECT SPOT TO LIE LOW FOR A TIME, JUST IN CASE THE COPS DO SMELL A RAT!
FUNNY THING ABOUT UNCLE! WE'RE THE ONLY ONES OF THE FAMILY LEFT ALIVE— JUST ME NOW— BUT I NEVER KNEW ANYTHING ABOUT HIM OR HIS BRANCH OF THE CRANDALLS! WELL, HE COULDN'T HAVE PICKED A BETTER TIME TO DIE!
LATER, AS HIS TRAIN NEARS HIS DESTINATION...
WONDER WHY UNCLE LIVED IN FORSAKEN COUNTRY LIKE THIS? I'LL MISS THE BRIGHT LIGHTS, BUT AT LEAST IT'S A LONG WAY FROM NEW YORK AND THE COPS! AND I DON'T HAVE TO STAY HERE FOREVER!
SOON HE GETS OFF AT A DESOLATE LITTLE STATION...
HEY, YOU! CAN YOU TAKE ME OUT TO THE OLD CRANDALL HOUSE?
RECKON I CAN, MISTER, IF YOU'RE DURNED FOOL ENOUGH TO WANT TO GO THERE! HOP IN!
SO YER CRANDALL'S NEPHEW, HUH? AND YOU AIM TO STAY AT THE HOUSE? I DON'T ENVY YOU NONE, YOUNG FELLER!
WHAT DO YOU MEAN? WHY ARE YOU BEING SO MYSTERIOUS ABOUT THE HOUSE?
BUT...
AIN'T GOT TIME TO TALK NOW! GETTING DARK, AND FUNNY THINGS HAPPEN AROUND HERE AFTER DARK! BE SEEIN' YOU, YOUNG FELLER— I HOPE!
WAIT A MINUTE, YOU FOOL! WHAT ARE YOU AFRAID OF? I DIDN'T EVEN PAY YOU!
3

EVEN CRANDALL HAS A SENSE OF GLOOMY FOREBODING AS HE APPROACHES THE RAMSHACKLE OLD MANOR HOUSE...

BRRR — I'M BEGINNING TO HATE THIS DUMP ALREADY! SOMETHING SPOOKY ABOUT IT — ONLY I DON'T BELIEVE IN SPOOKS! BUT I GUESS I CAN STAND IT A LITTLE WHILE!

HE SOON MAKES A DISCONCERTING DISCOVERY...

THE ELECTRICITY IS TURNED OFF, BLAST IT! NOTHING BUT DUST, COBWEBS AND RATS! IF IT WASN'T SUCH A PERFECT PLACE TO LIE LOW FOR A TIME, I'D LEAVE RIGHT NOW! BUT IT IS — SO I'LL MAKE THE BEST OF IT!

HEY, CANDLES! UGH — AND MORE RATS! GET AWAY, YOU! I'LL NEED THESE TONIGHT!

LATER, BY A ROARING FIRE, CRANDALL MAKES HIMSELF FAIRLY COMFORTABLE...

QUITE A COLLECTION OF BOOKS UNCLE HAD! THIS ONE IS A REAL LAUGH — A FAMILY HISTORY OF THE CRANDALLS! HAH-HAH! WONDER WHAT MY ANCESTORS WERE LIKE?

AND THEN CRANDALL READS SOMETHING THAT SENDS AN ICY SHIVER THROUGH HIM...

W-WHAT'S THIS? IT SAYS ONE OF MY ANCESTORS, A MAN NAMED ZACHARY CRANDALL, USED TO BE THE HANGMAN AROUND HERE! EVERYBODY HATED HIM! AND H-HERE'S A NOTE IN MY UNCLE'S HANDWRITING!

AND THIS H-HOUSE IS BUILT RIGHT OVER THE SITE OF THE OLD GALLOWS!

LATER, AS CRANDALL HUDDLES BETWEEN DANK SHEETS IN A MOULDY BEDROOM, HIS THOUGHTS RACE AROUND HIS BRAIN LIKE RATS IN A CAGE...

B-BLAST IT, WHY DID I READ THAT BOOK? I K-KEEP THINKING ABOUT H-HANGING! REMEMBERING H-HOW FERRIS LOOKED THAT NIGHT! IN A WAY I'M A H-HANGMAN, TOO!

AS THE HOUR OF TWELVE ARRIVES...

AHHYOOOOOO—

H-HUH! W-WHAT? I HEARD SOME-THING! I KNOW I DID! W-WHO—

YOWWWW— A G-GHOST!

EEEEGHHHH!

DO NOT FEAR ME! I ONLY COME TO WARN YOU, NOT TO HARM YOU!

LEAVE THIS PLACE! THIS GALLOWS' GROUND! HEE-HEE-HEE! THEY'LL HANG YOU, THE WAY THEY HANGED ME! I—HAH-HAH—WAS THE *HANGMAN*, BUT THEY *HANGED* ME TOO! ON THIS VERY SPOT! AND *YOU'RE* A HANGMAN! I KNOW—I KNOW! EEE—HEE-HEEEE!

GAAAAA— H-HOW DID YOU KNOW THAT?

WE KNOW— WE KNOW EVERY-THING! I'M THE GHOST OF THE HANGMAN, ZACHARY CRANDALL, AND I WARN YOU TO LEAVE THIS HOUSE! THIS HOUSE BUILT ON CURSED GALLOWS GROUND!

ZACHARY CRANDALL! HEY, WAIT! COME BACK AND TELL ME...

BUT AS THE GHOST OF OLD ZACHARY VANISHES, JASPER CRANDALL SEES SHADOWS CLOT AND FORM ON THE WALL! A CHILL WIND OF TERROR BLOWS DOWN HIS CRAVEN SPINE...

EEEEAAAAA— THE W-WALL! S-SHADOWS! A MAN—*HANGING*!

YOWWWEEE—

A STRANGE IMPULSE, LIKE A MAGNET OF FATE, DRAWS CRANDALL TOWARD THE WALL WHERE THE DREAD SHADOWS CAVORT...

STOP IT! LEAVE ME ALONE! LEAVE ME IN PEACE! YOU'RE NOTHING BUT SHADOWS, JUST SHADOWS! I KNOW I'M DREAMING, BUT I—(SOB)—CAN'T STAND IT! EEEEAAAAAAHHH— S-STOP THE HANGING!

SUDDENLY, LIKE THE TRAP IN A GALLOWS, SOMETHING GIVES WAY AND CRANDALL FALLS...

EEEEHHHHHH— F-FALLING! A TRAPDOOR! THEY'RE G-GOING TO H-HANG ME! — UNGGGGGGGG—

INTO A STRANGE LAND WHERE BLACK SILENCE BROODS AND TERROR RUNS THROUGH THE OBSCENE LANDSCAPE LIKE A SLIMY RIVER...

H-HUH? WHAT H-HAPPENED? WHERE AM I? I REMEMBER FALLING, THINKING THEY WERE HANGING ME, AND N-NOW...

SOON A DREADFUL SOUND FALLS UPON HIS EARS...

THOSE PEOPLE! THEY'RE ALL SHOUTING, CHEERING ABOUT SOMETHING! ONLY THEY DON'T S-SOUND VERY H-HAPPY! THEY SOUND —HORRIBLE!

YIIIII— GET ON WITH IT! — KILL HIM! — BLOOD — GIVE US BLOOD!

THEN CRANDALL UNDERSTANDS...

NOW I KNOW! IT'S A HANGING! THEY'RE GOING TO HANG THAT MAN IN THE CART! THAT'S WHY THEY'RE SO HAPPY! AND NOW, SUDDENLY, I'M HAPPY, TOO...

GNNNAAAAA—

I'M HAPPY, BECAUSE I'M GOING TO HELP! HAH-HAH-HAH! I'M A HANGMAN NOW, A REAL ONE! JUST LIKE MY ANCESTOR! AHH-HAH-HAH-HAH! OHH-HO-HOHO!

STOP SPINNING, YOU POOR FOOL! I —(CHUCKLE)— WANT TO SEE YOUR FACE! HAH-HAH! IT'S NO FUN TO HANG A MAN UNLESS YOU KNOW WHO IT IS YOU'RE HANGING! STOP, I SAY!

As the blubbering Crandall stares, he sees the body slow and jerk, running down like a dreadful clock...

GOOD! FINE! I'LL BE ABLE TO SEE THE FACE IN A MINUTE NOW! I MUST KNOW WHO IT IS THAT I HANGED! THERE—IT'S STOPPING!

EEEEEAAAAA— IT'S ME! I— I HANGED MYSELF!

And the terrible figures close in on him...

YOWWWEEEEE— LET ME GO! D-DON'T! I DIDN'T MEAN TO DO IT! I DIDN'T MEAN TO HANG MYSELF! GEEEEAAA—

HEH-HEH! (CACKLE)— "HANGED HIMSELF!"— HAH-HAH— HANG HIM AGAIN— AGAIN!

Until the trapdoor looms again...

THE T-TRAPDOOR AGAIN! GOT TO GET OUT! THAT'S IT! IF I CAN CRAWL BACK THROUGH IT, I'LL BE ALL RIGHT—NOT DEAD, NOT HANGED! G-GOT TO CLIMB BACK TO LIFE!

There is a thump and Jasper Crandall, sweating in agony, finds himself—on the floor beside his bed...

OHH—T-THANK GOODNESS! A DREAM! A HORRIBLE DREAM, BUT THAT'S ALL! B-BUT WAIT, SOMETHING IS WRONG WITH MY THROAT!

In a new sweat of terror, he stumbles toward a mirror...

MY THROAT IS ON FIRE! SO SORE, I CAN HARDLY SWALLOW! BUT WHAT, HOW? UNLESS I—BUT THAT'S CRAZY! IT WAS ONLY A NIGHTMARE!

Then, in the flickering light, Crandall sees something that makes his evil soul scream...

EEEEAYYYYYY— THE MARK OF THE ROPE!

CRINGING WITH TERROR, CRANDALL KNOWS WHAT HE MUST DO...

THAT DRIVER WAS RIGHT! YOU GOT TO BE CRAZY TO STICK AROUND THIS PLACE! IT'LL BE DAWN PRETTY SOON, AND I'M GETTING OUT! UGHH— BUILT RIGHT WHERE A GALLOWS USED TO STAND! NO WONDER PEOPLE HAVE NIGHTMARES!

AND WHAT A NIGHTMARE! I EVEN G-GOT THE ROPE MARK TO SHOW FOR IT! DREAMING THAT I HANGED MYSELF! I'VE GOT TO GET AWAY FROM HERE FAST, OR I'LL GO NUTS!

BUT AT THAT MOMENT, A RADIO ANNOUNCER IS MAKING AN ANNOUNCE- MENT THAT GREATLY CONCERNS CRANDALL...

WE INTERRUPT TO BRING YOU THIS IMPORTANT BULLETIN! FLASH — THE FIRST CYCLONE OF THE SEASON STRUCK WESTERN ARKANSAS TODAY! BE ON THE ALERT! THE WEATHER BUREAU AT LITTLE ROCK ADVISES THAT THIS IS A DANGEROUS TWISTER AND...

WHILE BACK IN THE FEAR-HAUNTED MANSION...

GAH— A C-CYCLONE! I'VE HEARD ABOUT THEM IN THIS COUNTRY! L-LOOKS LIKE I'M STUCK IN THIS CURSED PLACE FOR A TIME YET! BUT AT LEAST THE DAY IS COMING!

AND WITH THE DAWN'S COMING IS ALSO— DETECTIVE SERGEANT KOLB AND A FRIEND...

WE'RE GLAD TO COOPERATE, SERGEANT! HOW'D YOU HAPPEN TO NAIL THIS CRANDALL CHARACTER FOR THAT MURDER IN NEW YORK?

FUNNY THING! THE CORD THAT FERRIS WAS SUPPOSED TO HAVE USED TO HANG HIMSELF, DIDN'T HAVE A SINGLE FINGER-PRINT OF HIS! BUT CRANDALLS WERE ALL OVER IT! WE ALMOST MISSED IT!

YIII—GET THAT WIND! A CYCLONE MUST HAVE BLOWN UP!

WATCH IT, MAN! THE WIND— BLOWING US TOWARD THE EDGE!

8

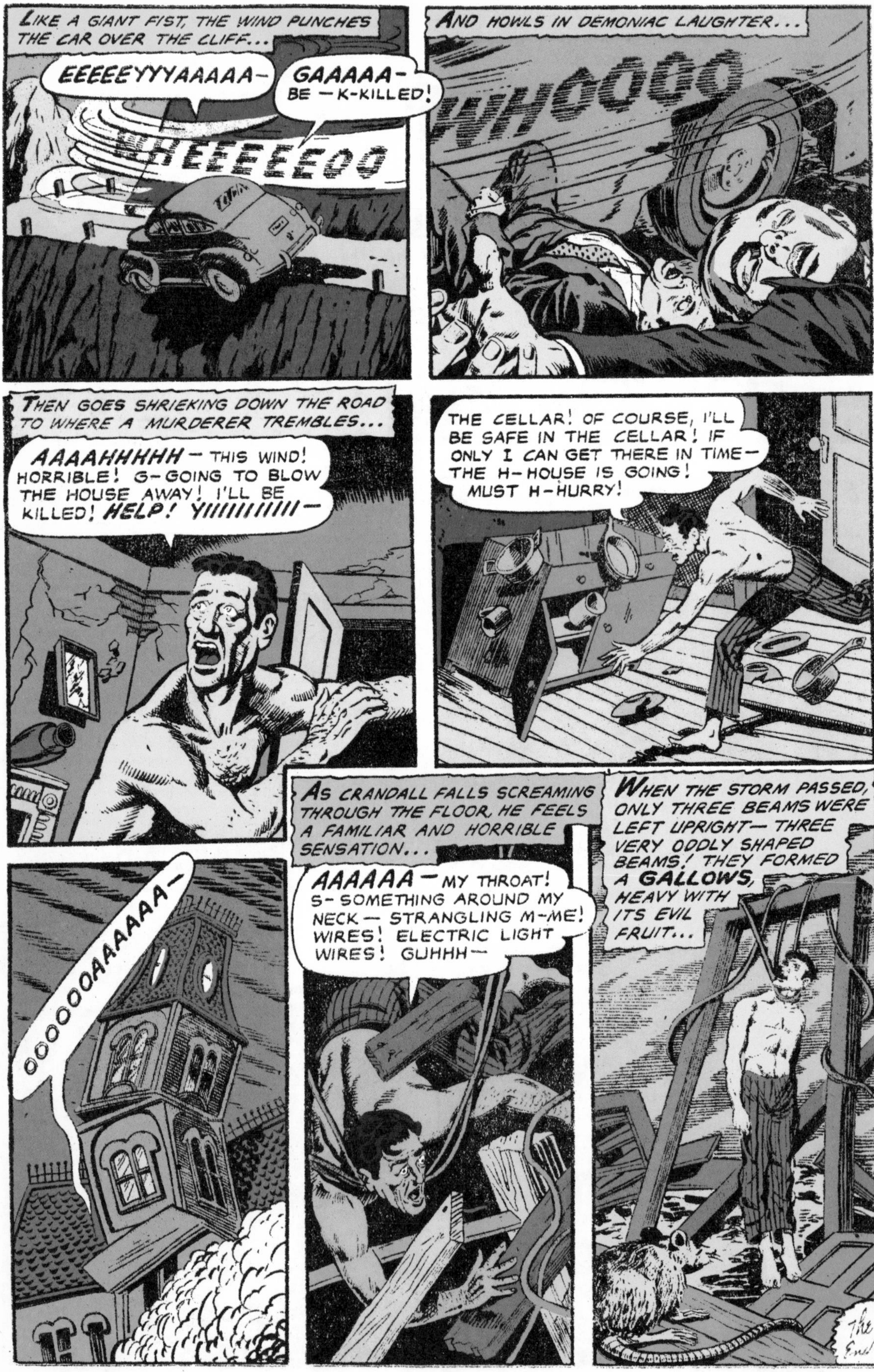
LIKE A GIANT FIST, THE WIND PUNCHES THE CAR OVER THE CLIFF...
EEEEEYYYAAAAA—
GAAAAA— BE —K-KILLED!
WHEEEEEEOO
AND HOWLS IN DEMONIAC LAUGHTER...
WHOOOOO
THEN GOES SHRIEKING DOWN THE ROAD TO WHERE A MURDERER TREMBLES...
AAAAHHHHH— THIS WIND! HORRIBLE! G-GOING TO BLOW THE HOUSE AWAY! I'LL BE KILLED! HELP! YIIIIIIIIIII—
THE CELLAR! OF COURSE, I'LL BE SAFE IN THE CELLAR! IF ONLY I CAN GET THERE IN TIME— THE H-HOUSE IS GOING! MUST H-HURRY!
OOOOOOAAAAAA—
AS CRANDALL FALLS SCREAMING THROUGH THE FLOOR, HE FEELS A FAMILIAR AND HORRIBLE SENSATION...
AAAAAA— MY THROAT! S-SOMETHING AROUND MY NECK— STRANGLING M-ME! WIRES! ELECTRIC LIGHT WIRES! GUHHH—
WHEN THE STORM PASSED, ONLY THREE BEAMS WERE LEFT UPRIGHT— THREE VERY ODDLY SHAPED BEAMS! THEY FORMED A GALLOWS, HEAVY WITH ITS EVIL FRUIT...
The End

WHAT DREAD CREATURE IS THIS, WHOSE PRESENCE IS A HORROR IN THE NIGHT? FROM WHAT PLACE OF TERROR BEYOND THE GRAVE DID THIS SKELETON-THING ARISE? WAS THERE NO WAY TO ESCAPE...

the RING of HORROR

B-1438

IN THE STUDY OF GORDON GRANT, STUDENT OF THE OCCULT...

I LOVE YOU, JANE. WILL YOU MARRY ME?

GORDON, DARLING... YOU *KNOW* I WILL!

YOU'RE *MINE* NOW... *FOREVER!*

YOU·· ...YOU SOUND SO *TENSE!* AND WHAT A STRANGE RING, LIKE A *KNOT* TWISTING ROUND MY FINGER!

JANE! THERE'S SOMETHING I MUST TELL YOU... ABOUT THIS RING... ABOUT US!

"ON MY LAST TRIP TO THE ORIENT, PURSUING MY STUDIES OF THE OCCULT, I WAS INITIATED INTO A STRANGE, LITTLE-KNOWN SECT CALLED "THE CULT OF THE BEAST"... I WAS THE FIRST NON-ORIENTAL THEY HAD EVER TAKEN IN, AND I WAS LOOKING FORWARD TO MAKING THEIR TEACHINGS KNOWN TO THE WESTERN WORLD, BUT WHEN THE INITIATION RITES WERE OVER..."

NOW THAT YOU ARE ONE OF US, YOU SHALL KNOW THE DREAD SECRET! LIKE ALL WHO WORSHIP THE BEAST, EXCEPT FOR ME, THE SACRED PRIEST... YOUR DAYS ON EARTH ARE NUMBERED! WITHIN A SPACE OF TIME THE BEAST WILL CLAIM YOU FOR HIS OWN!

BUT SO THAT YOU SHOULD NOT BE LONELY IN YOUR NEXT EXISTENCE, YOU MAY TAKE WITH YOU THE PERSON YOU MOST LOVE! TAKE THIS RING WITH THE KNOT OF THE BEAST! IT WILL BIND YOU AND YOUR BELOVED TOGETHER FOR ALL TIME!

SO NOW YOU KNOW, JANE... THE KNOT YOU WEAR BINDS US TOGETHER... FOR ALL TIME!

OH, GORDON, DARLING, YOUR STUDIES OF THE OCCULT HAVE MADE YOU MORBID! SURELY YOU DON'T BELIEVE THAT WEIRD TALE! IT'S JUST SUPERSTITION! THE RING *DOES* HAVE A STRANGE APPEARANCE... BUT I'M SURE IT HAS NO MYSTERIOUS POWER!

LET'S NOT BE SO SOLEMN! TELL YOU WHAT... WE'LL DRIVE UP TO TELL MY FAMILY THE GOOD NEWS ABOUT US... *NOW!*

DENSE FOG FILLED THE NIGHT WITH FOREBODING AS THEY DROVE ALONG...

GORDON, *DO* CHEER UP! WE OUGHT TO BE HAPPY TONIGHT, AND...

THEN OUT OF THE MISTS IT CAME... AS SWIFT AND CERTAIN AS... DEATH!

THE BEAST... IT'S COME FOR ME!

CRASH!

AGHHH!

...HEN THE MISTS CLEARED...

WHERE... WHAT'S HAPPENED? GORDON! **WHERE'S GORDON?**

DON'T TIRE YOURSELF, MISS MARSH! MR. GRANT IS...

DEAD! HE'S **DEAD!** ...THAT HORRIBLE IDOL I SAW BEFORE THE ACCIDENT...

NO...IT COULDN'T HAVE BEEN REAL! I...I JUST IMAGINED IT!

YOU'VE HAD A SHOCK, MISS MARSH! PLEASE TRY TO GET SOME REST, AND SOON YOU'LL STOP IMAGINING THINGS!

AFTER MONTHS OF MOURNING, JANE RETURNS TO WORK, BUT...

THE RING... GORDON'S RING... IT'S PRESSING MY FINGER AS THOUGH, IT WERE... **ALIVE!**

IT WON'T COME OFF! IT **CLINGS** AND **PRESSES**... WHY WON'T IT COME OFF?

I'VE GOT TO REMOVE IT... I'VE GOT TO!

FOREVER MINE JANE... REMEMBER! THE KNOT BINDS US TOGETHER... REMEMBER?

JANE HEARS GORDON'S LIFELESS VOICE, SEES HIS DISTORTED LIFELESS FACE...

YOU ARE MINE... YOU BELONG TO ME...

EVERYTHING GOES BLACK FOR JANE, THEN...

WHAT HAPPENED? YOU WENT OUT LIKE A LIGHT!

IT'S HER NERVES! LISTEN, THERE'S A **NEW DOCTOR** IN THIS BUILDING! YOU'D BETTER SEE HIM... **NOW!**

SOMEHOW, IN THE PRESENCE OF DR. WILL LYONS, THE PANIC SEEMS TO FADE...

I'M CERTAIN IT'S JUST... MY NERVES, DOCTOR! I'VE HAD A SHOCK LATELY AND...

BAD THINGS, JUMPY NERVES! SUPPOSE WE GIVE YOU SOMETHING TO MAKE YOU RELAX A BIT!

WITHIN A WEEK, THEY MEET AGAIN... BUT HARDLY ON A PROFESSIONAL BASIS...

IT'S BEEN A **WONDERFUL EVENING,** JANE! MIND IF I CALL YOU AGAIN?

I'D **LOVE** IT, WILL... **REALLY!** I HAVEN'T FELT SO WELL IN **AGES!** ALMOST ...HAPPY!

"**A**LMOST... HAPPY," JANE GOES TO SLEEP... BUT...

I HEARD A VOICE... **WHO IS IT? WHO'S THERE?**

HERE I AM, MY LOVE! I'LL NEVER LEAVE YOU! **I'LL BE WITH YOU... ALWAYS!**

YOU'RE NOT **REAL!** YOU'RE **DEAD,** GORDON ...DEAD!

NOT TO **YOU,** MY BELOVED! YOU WEAR MY RING, **THE KNOT OF ETERNITY!**

SO, TAKE HEED... **NO ONE ELSE MAY CLAIM YOU! NO ONE ELSE CAN HAVE YOU!** YOU... BELONG... TO... ME!

YOU'RE NOT *FICKLE*, ARE YOU, MY LOVE? YOU'RE NOT THINKING OF... *LEAVING ME*?

TAKE YOUR RING...LEAVE ME ALONE!

GOOD NIGHT, MY BELOVED. SLEEP WELL... DREAM OF ME ...*AND ONLY ME!*

SLEEP DID NOT COME TO JANE THAT NIGHT...

I'M LOSING MY MIND...THAT'S IT! I'M *INSANE!* THE SHOCK OF THE ACCIDENT... GORDON'S DEATH...BUT THESE WELTS ON MY WRIST, WHERE HE...IT...TOUCHED ME...

*A*SHAMED, FRIGHTENED, JANE DARED NOT SPEAK... EVEN TO WILL!

YOU SEEM TIRED, JANE! HAVEN'T YOU BEEN GETTING THE REST I PRESCRIBED?

NOT...NOT EXACTLY, WILL...BUT I'LL BE ALL RIGHT! IT'S NOTHING!

AMUSING PLAY, ISN'T IT?

IT'S *FOLLOWING ME* ...HAUNTING ME!

*O*NLY JANE'S EYES COULD SEE THE THING ...THE THING OF HORROR THAT CLAIMED HER...

YOU NEED SOMEONE TO LOOK AFTER YOU, JANE. A HUSBAND TO SEE...

NO, WILL, *NO!* DON'T TALK OF *MARRYING ME!*

BUT THIS IS A *PROPOSAL,* JANE! I LOVE YOU. I CAN *HELP* YOU, DARLING! WITH ME, YOU'LL GET WELL, BE HAPPY AGAIN...

OH, WILL. IT SOUNDS SO *WONDERFUL!*

IT WILL *BE* WONDERFUL! JUST SAY..."YES"!

YES, DARLING!

YOU NEVER REALLY LOVED HIM... THAT STRANGE MOODY MAN YOU WERE ENGAGED TO! I CAN TELL BY THE WAY YOU LOOK WHEN...

LET'S NOT *TALK* ABOUT HIM, WILL! LET'S TALK ABOUT *US!*

I HAVE ONLY ONE THING TO SAY. YOU'VE MADE ME VERY HAPPY!

I LOVE YOU. TOO, WILL... AS I NEVER THOUGHT I COULD!

SOON, WE'LL BE *TOGETHER*... WE WON'T HAVE TO PART AT THE DOOR! I'M SO *HAPPY...*

YES, JANE. BE HAPPY! WE *WILL* BE TOGETHER... SOON!

NOT YOU... NOT YOU... *YOU HORROR!*

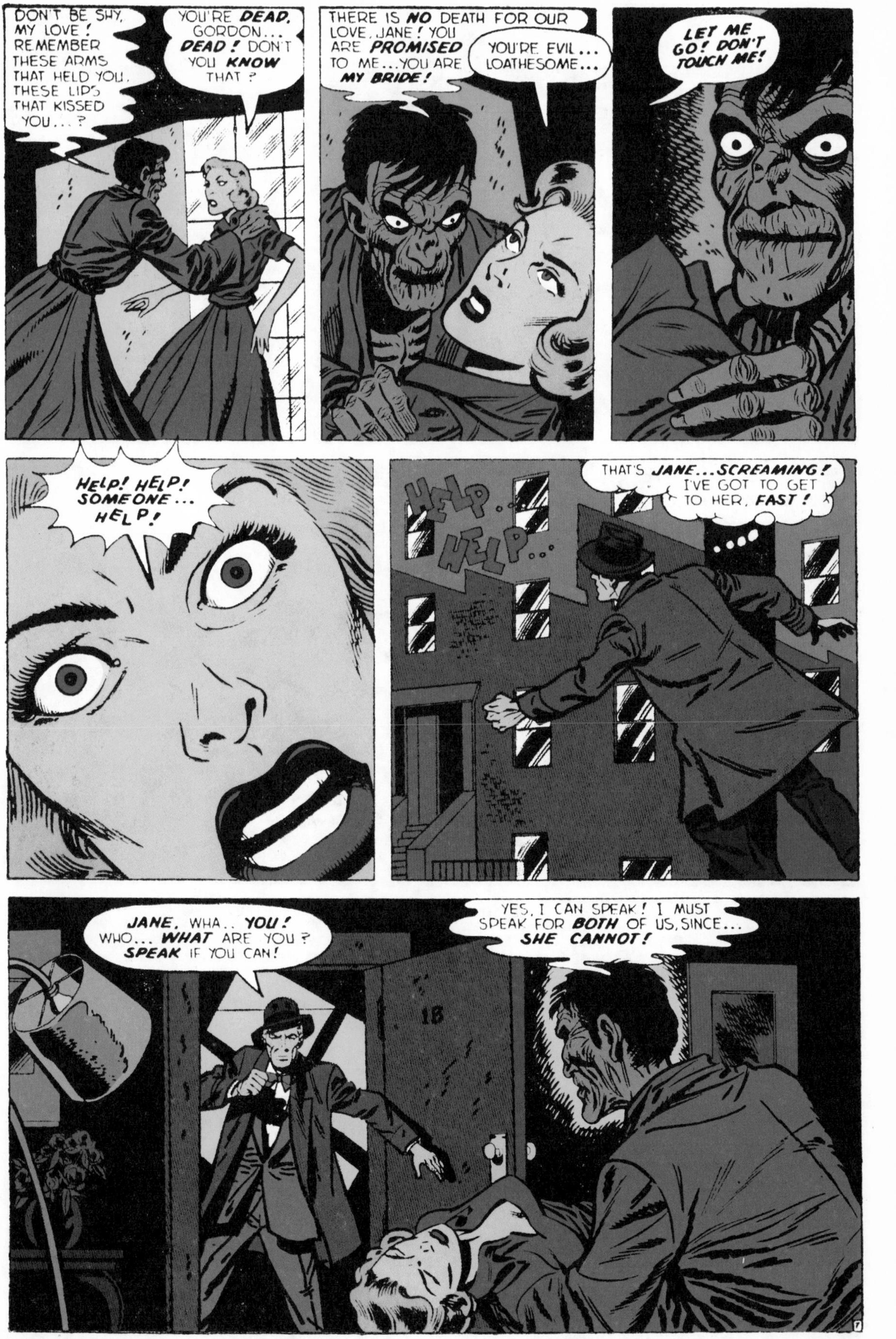
DON'T BE SHY, MY LOVE! REMEMBER THESE ARMS THAT HELD YOU, THESE LIPS THAT KISSED YOU...?
YOU'RE DEAD, GORDON... DEAD! DON'T YOU KNOW THAT?
THERE IS NO DEATH FOR OUR LOVE, JANE! YOU ARE PROMISED TO ME...YOU ARE MY BRIDE!
YOU'RE EVIL... LOATHESOME...
LET ME GO! DON'T TOUCH ME!
HELP! HELP! SOMEONE... HELP!
HELP...
HELP...
THAT'S JANE...SCREAMING! I'VE GOT TO GET TO HER, FAST!
JANE, WHA.. YOU! WHO... WHAT ARE YOU? SPEAK IF YOU CAN!
YES, I CAN SPEAK! I MUST SPEAK FOR BOTH OF US, SINCE... SHE CANNOT!
1B
7

YOU'VE *KILLED* HER! I DON'T KNOW WHAT YOU ARE OR WHERE YOU'VE COME FROM, BUT IF YOU'VE TAKEN HER LIFE...

HER LIFE WAS *MINE! SHE BELONGS TO ME*... AND *YOU* COULD NOT HAVE HER... *IN LIFE OR DEATH!*

I'LL TAKE HER FROM YOU... AND SAVE HER SOUL FROM YOUR CONTAMINATION!

YOU WAGE A LOSING FIGHT...

...A FIGHT AGAINST AN EVIL FORCE OLDER THAN TIME, ITSELF!

YOUR PUNY LITTLE LIFE HAS RUN ITS COURSE! NOW ...*DIE!*

TWO DEAD... THE STORY IS ENDED. BUT NOT QUITE! FOR TODAY, IN A SMALL SHOP WINDOW, ON A DUSTY TRAY, THERE IS A CURIOUS RING, TWISTED LIKE A KNOT! IF IT SHOULD STRIKE YOUR FANCY...

JEWELRY CURIOS-ANT

DON'T BUY IT!...HOVERING NEARBY, THE BEAST THAT WAS GORDON WAITS FOR SOMEONE ELSE TO WEAR THE RING...*HIS RING*... FOR, NOW THAT HE HAS JANE, HE WANTS STILL *MORE* COMPANIONS TO EASE THE LONLINESS OF HIS HORRIBLE, LINEARTHLY EXISTENCE!

The End.

HOUSE TO LET

I am Professor Raymond Janney. It is difficult, almost impossible to write... The pencil is so huge, and I am so tired. But my story must be told... it MUST!

—S.CHECK—

"FROM THE EARLIEST DAYS OF MY CAREER, I HAD BEEN FASCINATED BY THE ONE PROBLEM THAT SEEMED TO DEFY SOLUTION FOREVER!"

YOU'RE WASTING YOUR TIME, JANNEY! MAN WAS NEVER INTENDED TO SOLVE THAT PROBLEM, AND NEVER WILL!

PLEASE, DON'T BOTHER ME! LET ME CONCENTRATE ON MY WORK!

"AS THE YEARS PASSED, I BECAME EVEN MORE ABSORBED IN MY WORK..."

LOOK, GENTLEMEN! IN THIS TEST-TUBE IS EVERY ELEMENT FOUND IN LIVING THINGS...YET IT IS INERT, DEAD MATTER! WHY?

THAT'S SIMPLE, PROFESSOR JANNEY! IT JUST DOESN'T HAVE LIFE!

TRUE! BUT, CAN YOU TELL ME — WHAT IS LIFE?

"YES...THAT WAS THE MYSTERY I WAS DETERMINED TO PENETRATE...THE NATURE OF LIFE ITSELF!"

1

WHY...IT...IT'S A FORCE THAT WILL USE ANY MEANS TO PRESERVE ITSELF, AND GO ON LIVING!

EXACTLY! AND HAVE YOU EVER THOUGHT OF THE POSSIBILITIES FOR SCIENCE IF WE COULD PRODUCE THAT FORCE IN THE LABORATORY?

WE COULD ENDOW *ANYTHING* WITH LIFE... A PENCIL...A CHAIR... EVEN A STONE!

I GUESS SO! BUT EVERYONE KNOWS IT'S IMPOSSIBLE!

Impossible? I only wish it had been...for I have achieved it... and it has meant such unspeakable horror that...but I must go on with my story. There is so little time

"ONE NIGHT, AS I WAS WORKING IN MY LABORATORY AT HOME..."

THIS LAST INGREDIENT...A HITHERTO UNDISCOVERED FLUID DERIVED FROM LIVING PROTOPLASM...COMBINED WITH OTHER ELEMENTS...IT MAY WORK!

"SLOWLY, I POURED THE CONTENTS OF ONE TEST-TUBE INTO THE OTHER!"

THAT STRANGE BRILLIANCE... *IT...IT'S FOAMING OVER... FILLING THE ROOM!*

"THE ROOM WAS SUDDENLY ALIVE WITH A MILLION FLASHING, SHIMMERING COLORS...STRANGE VIBRATIONS HUMMED IN THE AIR... AND I FAINTED!"

"WHEN I REGAINED MY SENSES, I FELT THAT THERE WAS SOMETHING DIFFERENT ABOUT THE ROOM..." SOMETHING'S CHANGED...BUT *WHAT?* EVERYTHING *LOOKS* THE SAME!

"AND THEN...SUDDENLY...I *KNEW!* I WAS BEING *WATCHED*...STARED AT BY AN UNSEEN, MALEVOLENT BEING!" THERE'S SOMETHING... SOMEONE ELSE IN THIS ROOM WITH ME! I...I KNOW IT!

"IT TOOK A WHILE BEFORE THE FULL HORROR OF THE TRUTH DAWNED ON ME!" MY EXPERIMENT! IT WORKED! IT HAS MADE SOMETHING IN THIS ROOM ALIVE! BUT, WHAT? *WHAT?*

"WHATEVER IT WAS, I COULD FEEL THAT IT THREATENED MY LIFE, AND I RACED MADLY TO THE DOOR!" I KNOW I LEFT IT UN-LOCKED...AND NOW...I...CAN'T BUDGE IT! THE PHONE! I...I'LL SUMMON HELP TO GET ME OUT OF HERE!

THE WIRES...SEVERED! MUST TRY THE WINDOW! IT'S TRYING TO TRAP ME HERE...DESTROY ME!

"I DIDN'T FEEL THE FULL DESPAIR OF DOOM TILL I TRIED THE WINDOWS!" THEY'RE STUCK...EVERY ONE OF THEM...AND I CAN'T SMASH THEM...THEY'RE MADE OF SHATTER-PROOF GLASS IN CASE OF AN EXPLOSION RESULTING FROM ONE OF MY EXPERIMENTS!

"I WAS SEIZED WITH A SPASM OF UNREASON-ING PANIC THAT ALMOST DROVE ME MAD!" LET ME OUT! LET ME OUT! WHATEVER YOU ARE, LET ME OUT!

3

Once again I fainted. I know not how long I lay asleep, but when I awoke, an accidental glimpse into the mirror gave me the first inkling of the horror that confronted me.

I...I'M SHRINKING! IT...IT'S FEEDING ON ME..SUSTAINING ITS OWN EXISTENCE WITH MINE! AS IT CONSUMES MY LIFE FORCE, I'LL KEEP DWINDLING UNTIL I VANISH COMPLETELY!

"BY NOW, I HAD KNOWN THE ULTIMATE IN TERROR, AND I WAS DRAINED OF FEAR. I TRIED TO EXAMINE MY PREDICAMENT AND USE MY ABILITIES TO FIND A WAY OF SAVING MYSELF..."

I...I DON'T KNOW HOW MUCH TIME I HAVE BEFORE IT DESTROYS ME...BUT WHATEVER IT IS, I MUST TRY TO OUTWIT IT!

"FINALLY, I EVOLVED A SCHEME...YES, IT WAS DANGEROUS, AND MIGHT MEAN PAINFUL DEATH TO ME...BUT AT LEAST IT GAVE ME A CHANCE FOR SURVIVAL!"

I MUST COLLECT PAPERS FROM ALL OVER... PUT THEM IN A BIG HEAP!

ONCE THE HOUSE IS ON FIRE, HELP WILL COME FROM OUTSIDE. IT MAY BE TOO LATE...BUT I MUST TAKE THE CHANCE!

"HOWEVER, NO SOONER DID I LIGHT THE MATCH, THAN..."

THE WINDOW... OPENED BY ITSELF!

WHOOSH

"I RACED MADLY FOR THE WINDOW, BUT..."

NOW I UNDERSTAND! NOW I KNOW TO WHAT I HAVE GIVEN LIFE!

SLAMM!

IT...IT'S *MY HOUSE* THAT'S BECOME THIS LIVING, MALIGNANT BEING, FEEDING ON MY LIFE TO CONTINUE ITS OWN! AND WHEN I AM GONE, IT WILL CONTINUE TO FEED ON OTHERS!

I MUST MAKE A RECORD OF EVERYTHING THAT HAS HAPPENED, AND SAVE OTHERS FROM THE HORRIBLE HUNGER OF THE THING WHICH I CREATED!

"AS I GROW SMALLER, THE TASK BECOMES MORE AND MORE DIFFICULT!"

I AM RESIGNED TO MY OWN FATE... BUT I MUST SEE THAT MY STORY REACHES THE OUTSIDE WORLD. IF IT REMAINED HERE, THE HOUSE WOULD FIND SOME WAY TO DESTROY IT!

THERE MUST BE SOME WAY...YES... THAT LITTLE CREVICE IN THE WALL! THE HOUSE WILL FEED ON ME TILL I'M SMALL ENOUGH TO FIT THROUGH THAT CRACK...AND THEN I...I'LL TAKE MY STORY WITH ME!

SOON...SOON... IT WILL BE TIME!

AT THAT MOMENT, OUTSIDE PROFESSOR JANNEY'S HOUSE...

I'M TIRED OF HOUSE HUNTING, TOM! LET'S REST A WHILE HERE.

SURE, JOAN... JUST TAKE IT EASY...

SUDDENLY!

TOM! LOOK! A...A...I THINK IT'S A MOUSE RUNNING OUT OF THERE!

5

JOAN! LOOK OUT! A BRICK...TOPPLING FROM THE ROOF!

WHEW! THAT WAS A CLOSE CALL!

YES...BUT THAT POOR CREATURE...WHATEVER IT WAS...I...I'M AFRAID IT WAS DESTROYED! *LET'S GO!*

WAIT A SECOND, JOAN! THAT HOUSE...I HAVE A FEELING IT'S UNOCCUPIED. THERE'S NO HARM IN RINGING THE BELL!

HMMM...IT'S A NICE ENOUGH HOUSE...AND A PLEASANT LOCATION. WHY NOT TRY, AS LONG AS WE'RE HERE?

THERE'S SOMETHING ALMOST ALIVE ABOUT THIS HOUSE, TOM...AS IF IT HAS A PERSONALITY OF ITS OWN!

GO AHEAD. RING THE BELL. IF NO ONE ANSWERS, WE CAN PHONE AN AGENT AND SEE IF IT'S TO LET.

TOM...LOOK! THE DOOR SWUNG OPEN BY ITSELF...WHY...IT...IT'S ALMOST AS THOUGH IT'S WELCOMING US IN...ALMOST AS THOUGH IT *WANTS* US TO COME IN.

IT WON'T HURT JUST TO STEP IN THE LIVING ROOM AND TAKE A LOOK! COME ON, JOAN...

TOM! THE DOOR! IT...IT'S SLAMMED SHUT! SUDDENLY, I...I'M AFRAID!

SLAM!

YES, MANY TENANTS HAVE LIVED IN PROFESSOR JANNEY'S HOUSE SINCE THEN...BUT SOMEHOW THEY DON'T STAY LONG. ONE DAY, WHEN YOU'RE LOOKING FOR A NEW HOUSE TO MOVE TO...WHO KNOWS...EVEN YOU MAY OCCUPY THAT HOUSE...*FOR A WHILE!*

HOUSE TO LET

JOE MORRIS AND HIS WIFE, WHO RUN THE *OWL DINER* DOWN AT THE CORNER, KNOW THAT IN THE DARKEST HOURS OF THE MORNING, YOU CAN NEVER TELL WHAT OUTLANDISH FORMS ARE STIRRING IN THE DESERTED CANYONS OF THE CITY. IT WAS AT SUCH A TIME THEY FIRST SAW...

THE HUNGRY LODGER

B1081

IF BUSINESS DOESN'T PICK UP SOON, I DON'T KNOW WHAT WE'RE GOING TO DO, JOE.

SHH! HERE COMES A CUSTOMER!

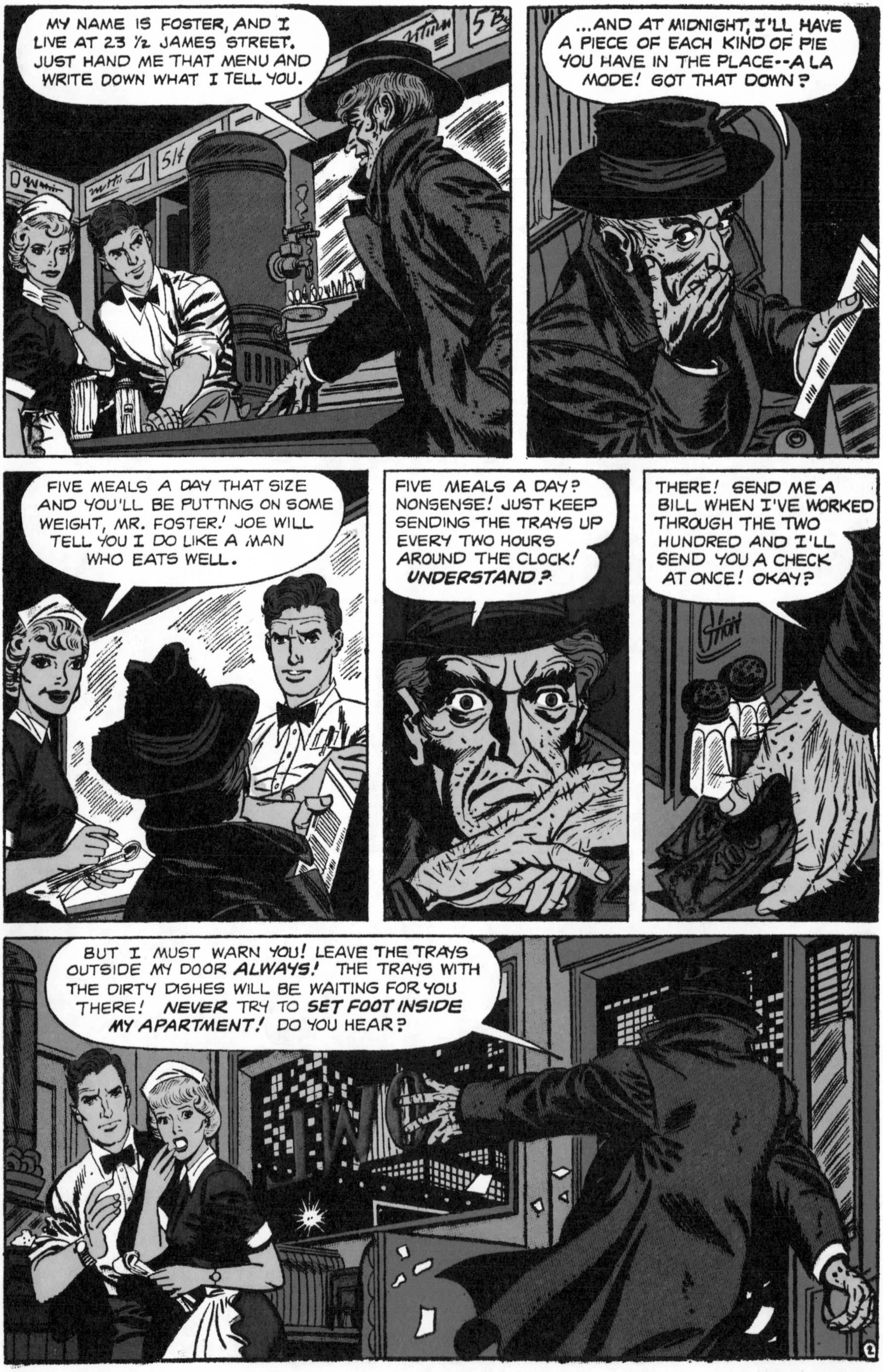
MY NAME IS FOSTER, AND I LIVE AT 23 ½ JAMES STREET. JUST HAND ME THAT MENU AND WRITE DOWN WHAT I TELL YOU.
...AND AT MIDNIGHT, I'LL HAVE A PIECE OF EACH KIND OF PIE YOU HAVE IN THE PLACE--A LA MODE! GOT THAT DOWN?
FIVE MEALS A DAY THAT SIZE AND YOU'LL BE PUTTING ON SOME WEIGHT, MR. FOSTER! JOE WILL TELL YOU I DO LIKE A MAN WHO EATS WELL.
FIVE MEALS A DAY? NONSENSE! JUST KEEP SENDING THE TRAYS UP EVERY TWO HOURS AROUND THE CLOCK! UNDERSTAND?
THERE! SEND ME A BILL WHEN I'VE WORKED THROUGH THE TWO HUNDRED AND I'LL SEND YOU A CHECK AT ONCE! OKAY?
BUT I MUST WARN YOU! LEAVE THE TRAYS OUTSIDE MY DOOR ALWAYS! THE TRAYS WITH THE DIRTY DISHES WILL BE WAITING FOR YOU THERE! NEVER TRY TO SET FOOT INSIDE MY APARTMENT! DO YOU HEAR?
2

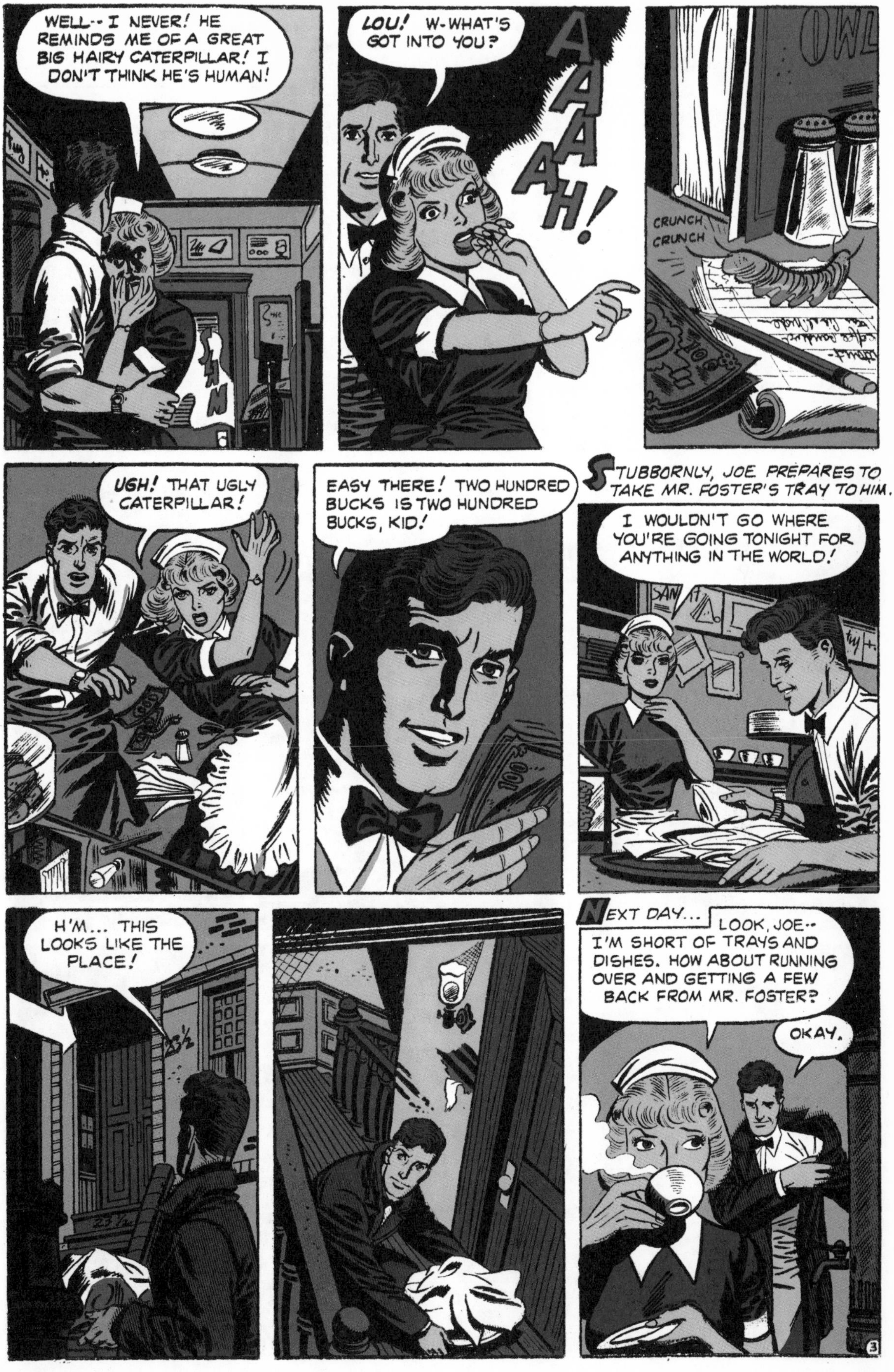
WELL-- I NEVER! HE REMINDS ME OF A GREAT BIG HAIRY CATERPILLAR! I DON'T THINK HE'S HUMAN!
LOU! W-WHAT'S GOT INTO YOU?
AAAAAH!
CRUNCH CRUNCH
UGH! THAT UGLY CATERPILLAR!
EASY THERE! TWO HUNDRED BUCKS IS TWO HUNDRED BUCKS, KID!
STUBBORNLY, JOE PREPARES TO TAKE MR. FOSTER'S TRAY TO HIM.
I WOULDN'T GO WHERE YOU'RE GOING TONIGHT FOR ANYTHING IN THE WORLD!
H'M... THIS LOOKS LIKE THE PLACE!
23½
NEXT DAY...
LOOK, JOE-- I'M SHORT OF TRAYS AND DISHES. HOW ABOUT RUNNING OVER AND GETTING A FEW BACK FROM MR. FOSTER?
OKAY.
3

BUT JOE WAS NOT EXPECTING THE SHOCKING SIGHT THAT AWAITED HIM!

I'VE GOT TO KILL THEM ALL! LOU MUST NEVER KNOW ABOUT THIS!

AND SO, FOR A TIME, JOE FOUGHT DOWN HIS LOATHING AND CARRIED OUT MR. FOSTER'S INSTRUCTIONS. BUT ONE DAY...

GOOD GRIEF! I FORGOT TO LEAVE A NOTE ON THE TRAY FOR MR. FOSTER. I'LL HAVE TO GO BACK!

A-A-R-GH!

LET ME OUT OF HERE!

PLEASE! UPSTAIRS! COME QUICK! SOMETHING STRANGE -- COME QUICK!

POLICE! MR. FOSTER! OPEN UP!

GET THE POLICE EMERGENCY UNIT HERE! WE DON'T KNOW WHAT WE'LL FIND!

CRASH!

4

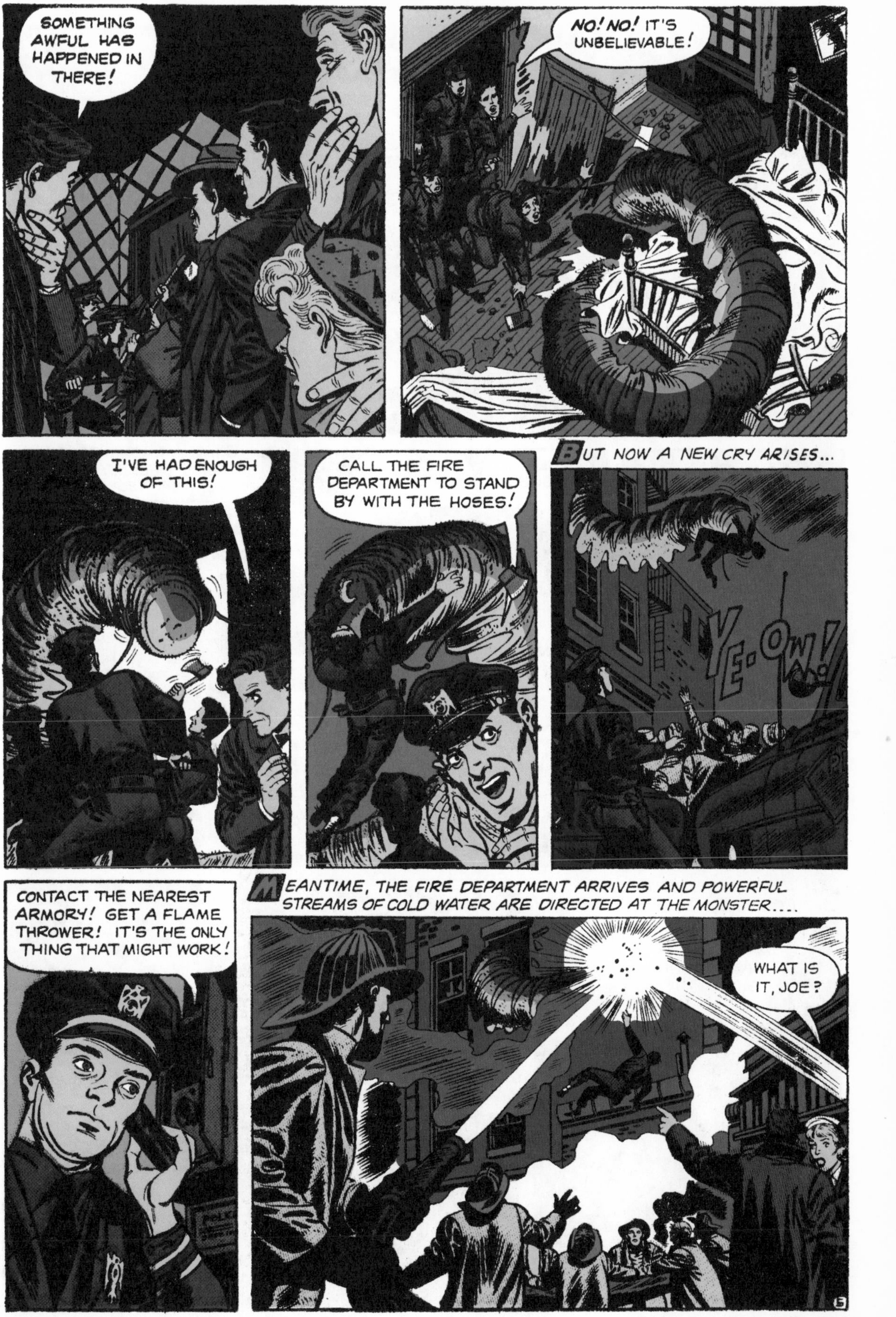
SOMETHING AWFUL HAS HAPPENED IN THERE!
NO! NO! IT'S UNBELIEVABLE!
I'VE HAD ENOUGH OF THIS!
CALL THE FIRE DEPARTMENT TO STAND BY WITH THE HOSES!
BUT NOW A NEW CRY ARISES...
YE-OW!
CONTACT THE NEAREST ARMORY! GET A FLAME THROWER! IT'S THE ONLY THING THAT MIGHT WORK!
MEANTIME, THE FIRE DEPARTMENT ARRIVES AND POWERFUL STREAMS OF COLD WATER ARE DIRECTED AT THE MONSTER....
WHAT IS IT, JOE?
5

HERE ARE THE FLAME THROWERS!

A SCENE FOLLOWS THAT IS STRAIGHT FROM THE INFERNAL REGIONS!

THERE IT GOES!

IT'S WEAKENING!

GIVE IT ANOTHER DOSE!

AND NOW THE BEAST DROPS LIFELESS FROM THE CHARRED POST...

'RAY!

THUD

AFTER IT IS ALL OVER, JOE MORRIS ASKS HIS WIFE A QUESTION.

BUT WHERE IS MR. FOSTER? HAS ANYONE SEEN HIM?

LOOK! THERE HE IS! THE CATERPILLAR—!

THE END

THINK OF A NIGHTMARE IN WHICH SOME NAMELESS HORROR DRAGS YOU OFF SCREECHING, TO SOME DREAD DOOM...THINK OF THIS NIGHTMARE OCCURRING AGAIN AND AGAIN! SUCH WAS THE GHASTLY NIGHTMARE THAT VISITED A YOUNG COUPLE....A NIGHTMARE FROM WHICH THEY COULD NOT WAKE! YOU SEE, IT WAS ALL **REAL** AND THERE WAS **NO ESCAPE FROM**......

The NINE HORRORS

TH-THE NINE HORRORS! BUT THEY'RE ALL *PHANTOMS*... EXCEPT *ONE!* WE'RE LOST UNTIL WE KILL THE *RIGHT* ONE!

BUT WHICH ONE? *WHICH* ONE?

B-1088

SOCIAL I...

Roger Kingsmith noted sportsman big game hunter and his bride the former Betty Templeton are spending their honeymoon at Mr. Kingsmith private hunt lodge.

Kingsmith you know just retu an expedi the jung India in of Kazl

The Roger Kingsmith tographed while tiger travels.

AT THE SECLUDED WOODLAND HUNTING LODGE, ROGER KINGSMITH POINTS WITH PRIDE AT HIS LATEST TROPHY...

YES, DEAR, THAT'S THE BIGGEST MALE TIGER EVER BAGGED --IN INDIA, OF COURSE, PROVINCE OF KAZHLAH! ISN'T IT MAGNIFICENT?

KAZHLAH? ISN'T THAT THE REGION WHERE THEY HAVE THE STRANGE LEGEND OF THE *CAT PEOPLE?* PEOPLE WHO TURN INTO *PREYING TIGERS?*

OH NONSENSE, SWEETHEART! WHO BELIEVES IN POPPY-COCK LIKE THAT? WHY, YOU'RE TREM-BLING, DEAR!

I-I CAN'T HELP IT, DARLING! WHAT IF IT'S TRUE? IT GIVES ME THE SHUDDERS TO THINK OF IT!

WH-WHAT'S *THAT...* THOSE FIERCE GREEN EYES...!

BETTY, GET HOLD OF YOUR NERVES!

IT'S ONLY SYVVA, OUR NEW HOUSE-KEEPER! WHAT MADE YOU JUMP LIKE THAT?

I---I---BUT SHE CAME UP SO SILENTLY, WITHOUT A SOUND! FORGIVE ME, ROGER! IT WAS SILLY OF ME, I KNOW!

I MUST CONFESS, ROGER---I DON'T LIKE HER! LOOK HOW SHE WALKS---WITH FELINE GRACE! HER GREEN EYES CAN FLASH FIRE AND SHE ALMOST HISSES WHEN ANGRY. AND ONCE SHE SEEMED TO PURR IN FRONT OF THE FIRE! GET RID OF HER, DEAR...PLEASE!

BUT DARLING! HOUSEKEEPERS ARE HARD TO GET IN THIS OUT-OF-WAY NECK OF THE WOODS!

AFTER MY LAST TRIP BACK FROM INDIA, IT TOOK WEEKS TO FIND A WOMAN AND I WAS GLAD TO GET SYVVA! DEAREST, YOUR NERVES ARE JITTERY! WHY DON'T YOU GO TO BED AND FORGET IT? I'LL SMOKE ONE MORE PIPE!

ALL RIGHT, DEAR! MAYBE I'M JUST ON EDGE!

PEACEFULLY SMOKING AT THE FIRE BEFORE RETIRING, ROGER IS SUDDENLY SHOCKED BY A PIERCING SCREAM FROM UP-STAIRS!

EEEAAA! ROGER! HELP!

BETTY! WHAT IN THUNDER--?

IN THE BEDROOM...

EEAAAA--TIGER!

GREAT HEAVENS!

IN DESPERATE HASTE, ROGER RETRIEVES A HUNTING RIFLE FROM THE HALL AND...

MISSED IN THE DARK! BUT THAT SCARES IT OFF ANYWAY!

KA POW

2.

DID I DREAM IT ALL? IT'S FANTASTIC---A WILD TIGER HERE IN AMERICA!

EH? SYVVA? DID YOU SEE A TIGER? AND WHAT THE DEVIL ARE YOU DOING OUT HERE AT NIGHT?

JUST GETTING FRESH AIR, SIR! I SAW NO TIGER. PARDON ME, BUT ISN'T THAT RIDICULOUS?

EVERYONE KNOWS TIGERS DO NOT EXIST IN AMERICA, EXCEPT IN ZOOS! PERHAPS IT WAS YOUR IMAGINATION? OR A MOCKING SHADOW? I'M CERTAIN THERE IS NO TIGER LOOSE AROUND HERE!

HMM, I--I GUESS YOU'RE RIGHT, SYVVA. BETTY AND I BOTH VISIONED A MYTHICAL TIGER IN THE DARK. GOOD NIGHT!

BUT IT WAS REAL, ROGER! I SAW ITS GLEAMING TEETH... HORRIBLE GREEN EYES... RAKING CLAWS....

NOW, NOW, MY DEAR! SHEER HALLUCINATION! WE'LL SLEEP IT OFF AND TOMORROW WE'LL LAUGH AT OURSELVES!

THE NEXT MORNING, IN THE CLEAR LIGHT OF DAY, THE EXPERIENCE OF THE NIGHT BECOMES A MATTER OF HILARITY FOR THE HONEYMOON COUPLE, THEIR GOOD SPIRITS RETURNING.

HOW SILLY WE WERE LAST NIGHT! LET'S SING AND LAUGH AND BE GAY TODAY, DARLING!

SURE THING, BETTY! BUT AN IMAGINARY TIGER...I CAN'T HELP LAUGHING NOW...

ROGER, WHAT'S WRONG? HAVE YOU SEEN A GHOST?

IT'S WORSE THAN A GHOST ---THESE ARE TIGER PRINTS!

THE TIGER, OHHH!

IN BROAD DAYLIGHT! IT CAN'T BE OUR IMAGINATION THIS TIME!

ONLY ONE CHANCE...STRAIGHT BETWEEN THE EYES...STEADY...

YOU GOT HIM, ROGER! THANK HEAVEN!

BLAM!

NOT HIM, BETTY! THAT'S A FEMALE ---A TIGRESS!

BUT WHAT DOES IT ALL MEAN, ROGER? WHERE DID A WILD TIGRESS COME FROM? WHY DID IT STALK US? IT'S SO... INSANE!

UNNERVED BY THE EXPERIENCE, BETTY IS ALMOST IN A STATE OF COLLAPSE WHEN THEY RETURN TO THE LODGE...

SYVVA, QUICKLY! TAKE CARE OF MY WIFE! SHE'S IN A STATE OF SHOCK! WE JUST KILLED A TIGER!

TIGER, SIR?

RIDICULOUS, SIR! TIGERS ARE UNKNOWN IN THIS LAND! YOU ARE BOTH MAKING UP SILLY STORIES!

THAT'S ENOUGH, SYVVA! ARE YOU CALLING US LIARS? I TELL YOU I SAW AND SHOT A HUGE TIGRESS DEAD!

PAH! I STILL DON'T BELIEVE IT!

ALL RIGHT, YOU STUBBORN FOOL! I'LL GO BACK TO THE DEAD CARCASS AND BRING BACK THE HEAD! I WANT IT AS A TROPHY ANYWAY!

BLAST THAT WOMAN! SHE GOT UNDER MY SKIN WITH HER SNEERING! I'LL BRING BACK THAT HEAD AND RAM IT DOWN HER THROAT! CALL ME A LIAR, WILL SHE?

BUT WHEN HE RETURNS TO THE SPOT, ROGER IS STUNNED BY THE MOST UNCANNY SURPRISE OF ALL...

NO CARCASS? BUT IT WAS RIGHT HERE! HOW COULD IT VANISH INTO THIN AIR?

WAIT--THERE'S ONE GHASTLY EXPLANATION FOR IT ALL! WHY DID I FIND SYVVA, THE HOUSE-KEEPER, IN THE MOONLIGHT LAST NIGHT, AFTER THE TIGRESS ATTACKED AND FLED? AND WHY DID SYVVA GOAD ME ON TO COME HERE AND PROVE I KILLED A TIGRESS? AND WHY DIDN'T I FIND THE DEAD CAR-CASS?...GREAT SCOTT...NOW I SEE!

IT'S MAD--IMPOSSIBLE--BUT WHAT IF IT'S TRUE? AND I LEFT BETTY ALONE WITH SYVVA!

MEANWHILE, AT THE LODGE, BETTY HAS ALSO ADDED TWO AND TWO TO GET A HORRIFYING FOUR!

≷SPIT!--SPIT!≷ I'VE GOT YOU ALONE!

SYVVA--I KNEW IT--FELT IT-- Y-YOU'RE A CAT WOMAN!

4

SO YOU FINALLY FIGURED IT OUT? YES, AND NOW YOU SHALL DIE! THAT'S MY REVENGE AGAINST ROGER---KILLING HIS BRIDE!

I'M LOST, UNLESS I STALL HER....

BUT WHY? WHAT DID ROGER EVER DO TO YOU?

...ALL RIGHT, HEAR MY STORY! ROGER HUNTED IN KAZHLAH, MY HOME PROVINCE, STALKING AND KILLING THE BIGGEST MALE TIGER OF THE REGION, A MAN-EATER FOR YEARS!

AMONG US CAT PEOPLE, THAT TIGER WAS MY *MATE!* ALL NIGHT LONG, UNDER THE DREARY MOON, I MOURNED MY LOVE!

...BEFORE DAWN, WHEN I KNEW ROGER WOULD COME, I LEFT AND MADE A RELENTLESS VOW......

REVENGE! REVENGE AGAINST THE KILLER OF MY MATE! I WILL HOUND HIM TO THE ENDS OF THE EARTH! SOME- WHERE...SOMEHOW... SOMEDAY...I WILL HAVE MY VENGEANCE!

AND NOW, WHAT SWEETER REVENGE THAN TO KILL *HIS* BELOVED···YOU! WATCH ME CHANGE BEFORE YOUR EYES, INTO A CLAWING, SLASHING, RAGING TIGRESS!

NO... NO!

THE NEXT MOMENT, BEFORE BETTY'S EYES, THE MERCILESS TIGRESS TAKES FORM AND LEAPS...BUT....

ROGER! JUST IN TIME!

BANG! SNARL-YEOW WWW!

I STALLED HER LONG ENOUGH FOR YOU TO GET BACK!

SMART THINKING, DEAREST! SHE'S ONLY WOUNDED-- SHE'S GETTING AWAY! BUT IT'S A MORTAL WOUND, NEAR THE HEART!

SHE'LL DIE IN THE WOODS! THE DANGER IS ALL OVER!

NO, IT ISN'T, ROGER! DON'T YOU UNDERSTAND? DON'T YOU SEE THE SIGNIFICANCE OF ALL THIS? DIDN'T YOU SHOOT AND KILL THE TIGRESS, NOT ONCE, BUT TWICE?

YOU... YOU MEAN--?

YES! DON'T YOU REMEMBER THE OLD SAYING THAT ALL CATS HAVE.... NINE LIVES?

WITH THESE FRIGHTFUL CAT PEOPLE, INVESTED WITH UNHOLY SUPERNATURAL POWERS, THE LEGEND IS TRUE! YOU ONLY KILLED HER TWICE....

SEVEN TIMES TO GO! I'VE GOT TO DO THE MESSY JOB OVER AND OVER, NINE TIMES IN ALL, BEFORE WE'RE SAFE!

THE GRIM HUNT BEGINS.....

SORRY, DEAR! YOU HAVE TO BE MY GUN-BEARER AND ALSO KEEP SCORE FOR ME. I HAVE TO KILL THE TIGRESS SEVEN MORE TIMES ---THE SAME ONE!

OVER AND OVER, AS IF IN A NEVER-ENDING NIGHTMARE, THE HUNTER STALKS AND KILLS HIS QUARRY!

OVER AND OVER....

HOW MANY TIMES, BETTY? IT SEEMS LIKE I'VE BEEN SHOOTING FOR ALL ETERNITY!

ONLY FIVE TIMES, DARLING! COURAGE! FOUR MORE TIMES TO GO!

IT WAS MAD, INSANE, UNEARTHLY, BUT FINALLY....

THE NINTH AND LAST TIME, ROGER! DON'T MISS!

NO--- NO! THE GUN--- EMPTY!

THAT WAS THE *LAST OF MY AMMUNITION!* QUICK, BACK TO THE LODGE, OR WE'RE SUNK! THE CAT WOMAN HAS *ONE MORE LIFE* TO GO!

BUT NOW, THE HUNTERS BECOME THE HUNTED, AS A VENGEFUL TAWNY FORM STALKS THEM WITH HUMAN CUNNING!

I HEARD THE CLICK OF THE EMPTY GUN! I'LL RUN THEM DOWN NOW BEFORE THEY REACH THE LODGE!

ROGER-- ROGER! OH, WHY DID YOU LEAVE ME?

SO HE TURNED COW-ARD AND LEFT HER ALONE! PERFECT! I'LL GET THEM ONE AT A TIME---THE GIRL FIRST!

BUT A SILENT NOOSE DROPS FROM THE TREE ABOVE....

AN OLD HUNTING TRICK, MY TIGRESS FRIEND! BETTY WAS THE LURING "BAIT," HELPLESS AND ALONE, WHILE I WAITED UP HERE!

DEAD--FOR THE NINTH AND FINAL TIME! OUR ENEMY IS GONE....FOR-EVER!

OH, DARLING! IT WAS HORRIBLE.... DREADFUL....!

LATER.... HER MATE, THE MAN-KILLER, HAD EVIDENTLY BEEN HUNTED AND KILLED EIGHT TIMES BE-FORE, WHEN I SHOT HIM THE NINTH TIME! SO BOTH THOSE UNCANNY CAT PEOPLE ARE NOW JUST---TROPHIES!

YES, TROPHIES OF TERROR! PROMISE ME ONE THING, DARLING---NEVER HUNT IN KAZLAH AGAIN!

THE END

THE LITTLE CHILDREN

A TALE OF HORROR

THAT'S AL SOMMER'S HOUSE...THE SECOND ONE FROM THE CORNER. NEAT LITTLE JOB, ISN'T IT? NICE LITTLE FAMILY HOUSE. AL'S AT THE BREAKFAST TABLE RIGHT NOW... SIPPING HIS COFFEE, FLIPPING THROUGH THE MORNING PAPER...

AL, WHAT'S THE MATTER? YOUR HANDS ARE SHAKING!

CLARA... IT'S HAPPENED AGAIN!

TWELFTH MYSTERY EXPLOSION

H-HOW MANY PEOPLE KILLED THIS TIME, AL?

OVER FOUR HUNDRED. JUST LIKE ALL THE OTHERS. A HEAVILY GUARDED INDUSTRIAL PLANT GOING AT FULL BLAST, THEN ALL OF A SUDDEN... *BOOM!* EVERYBODY AND EVERYTHING WENT SKY-HIGH!

AL, YOU'RE NOT BLAMING YOURSELF... ARE YOU? THERE MUST BE A THOUSAND DETECTIVES ALL OVER THE WORLD WORKING ON THESE CASES! AL... DO YOU HEAR ME?

I HEAR YOU, CLARA. I HEAR YOU. I JUST WANT TO SEE IF JOHNNY'S ALL RIGHT.

AL BENDS OVER THE BED WHERE LITTLE JOHNNY LIES SLEEPING. CUTE LITTLE KID, JOHNNY. AL AND CLARA FELL FOR HIM LIKE A TON OF BRICKS THE FIRST TIME THEY SAW HIM AT THE ORPHANAGE. AFTER EIGHTEEN CHILDLESS YEARS, AT LAST. THEY HAD A KID OF THEIR OWN!

IT WORKS EVERY TIME! EVERY TIME I FEEL BLUE, ALL I HAVE TO DO IS TAKE A PEEK AT JOHNNY, AND I'M WALKING ON CLOUDS AGAIN...

CRAZY ABOUT HIM, AREN'T YOU, AL? HONEY, I HATE TO RUSH YOU, BUT IT'S TIME YOU LEFT FOR WORK.

WHEN I THINK OF THOSE EIGHTEEN YEARS, CLARA, AND LOOK DOWN AT JOHNNY... I-I SORT OF CHOKE UP INSIDE... I FEEL SO GOOD! YEAH.. GIVE ME MY HAT, SWEETHEART, AND KISS JOHNNY FOR ME WHEN HE WAKES UP.

WHEN AL GETS TO WORK...

HI, CHIEF!

SEE THE PAPER THIS MORNING, AL?

YEAH. SAW ALL OF THEM ON THE WAY DOWN. I GOT THE WHOLE ROTTEN PICTURE. FOUR HUNDRED AND THIRTY SIX DEAD. BUT NOT EVEN ONE LIKELY SUSPECT.

AL, THAT'S THE TWELFTH EXPLOSION IN TWO WEEKS! JAMMED-FULL FACTORIES BLOWING SKY-HIGH ALL OVER THE WORLD! IT HAS TO STOP!

SURE, *IT HAS TO STOP!* BUT NOBODY CAN PIN ANY BLAME ON *US* RIGHT HERE! WE'RE *ONE* MIDDLE-SIZED POLICE FORCE IN *ONE* MIDDLE-SIZED AMERICAN CITY! WHAT CAN WE DO?

YOU'RE RIGHT, AL... SORRY I BLEW OFF STEAM. IT'S JUST ...THAT I'M SCARED, I GUESS. JUST KEEP DOING YOUR JOB, AL. TRACK DOWN EVERY LEAD THAT TURNS UP. THAT'S ALL ANY OF US CAN DO.. KEEP DOING HIS JOB...

SO AL SITS DOWN AT HIS DESK AND HE'S JUST BEGUN CHEWING AT HIS FIRST CIGAR OF THE DAY WHEN THE PHONE RINGS...

A MISS HERMIONE LAURENTS TO SEE YOU, AL. LOOKS LIKE A SCREWBALL. SAYS SHE HAS THE INSIDE DOPE ON ALL THOSE EXPLOSIONS.

I BET SHE EVEN KNOWS ALL ABOUT WHY THE COW JUMPED OVER THE MOON. AAAH... SEND HER IN. IF THE CHIEF HEARS I TURNED ANY LEAD AWAY, HE'D CHEW MY HEAD OFF.

MR. SOMMER...YOU MUST LISTEN! NO ONE ELSE WILL! THEY ALL LAUGH! BUT YOU MUST LISTEN!

RELAX, LADY! TAKE A SEAT. I'LL LISTEN. BUT MAKE IT SHORT AND SWEET, HUH... THIS IS ON TAXPAYER'S MONEY...

I AM A MYSTIC, MR. SOMMER! I OWN A VAST LIBRARY OF OCCULT BOOKS! AND I KNOW ALL ABOUT THOSE DEMONS WHO 'TIL NOW HAVE LIVED DEEP, DEEP DOWN IN THE CORE OF THE EARTH...

"IT HAS ALWAYS BEEN THEIR AMBITION TO BREAK THROUGH TO THE SURFACE! THEY ARE EVIL, MR. SOMMER'S ...HORRIBLY EVIL! BUT THEY ARE CLEVER AND SINCE THE BEGINNING OF TIME, THEY HAVE BEEN PONDERING WAYS AND MEANS OF CONQUERING MAN....

...THEY KNOW, OF COURSE, THAT IF THEY SHOW THEM-SELVES ON THE SURFACE IN THEIR OWN HIDEOUS FORMS, THEIR EVIL INTENT WILL BE IMMEDIATELY APPARENT! SO THEY HAVE ENTERED THE BODIES OF INNOCENT CHILDREN!

"AND AS INNOCENT CHILDREN, THEY HAVE BEEN WALKING BY UNSUSPECTING GUARDS AT INDUSTRIAL PLANTS, CARRYING THEIR POWERFUL BOMBS!

THEY PLAN TO TAKE OVER THE WHOLE WORLD MR. SOMMER. BUT THERE IS A CHINK IN THEIR ARMOR! THEY HAVE RENDERED THEMSELVES VULNERABLE BY APPEARING IN THEIR DISGUISE! FOR IF JUST ONE OF THEM IS RECOGNIZED AND, IMMEDIATELY KILLED, ALL OF THEM WILL PERISH!

BUT ON THE OTHER HAND, IF ONE IS RECOGNIZED AND *NOT* KILLED IMMEDIATELY, THEN BY THE SAME TOKEN, THE WORLD WILL BE THEIRS BY DEFAULT! SO....

WHOOOA, LADY! YOU'VE BEEN TALKING A MILE A MINUTE! NOW LET'S ASSUME JUST FOR ARGUMENT'S SAKE THAT YOU HAVE THE RIGHT DOPE...

WOULD YOU MIND TELLING A GUY JUST HOW TO GO ABOUT RECOGNIZING ONE OF THESE... WHATDOYOUCALLTHEM...DEMONS?

YOU WILL KNOW INSIDE! A VOICE INSIDE YOUR HEART WILL TELL YOU! MR. SOMMER... YOU'RE SMILING! YOU DON'T BELIEVE ME! BUT YOU *MUST*! YOU... AIEEE!

LADY, YOU'VE WASTED ENOUGH OF MY TIME. NOW SKIDOO BEFORE I CALL THE MAN IN THE WHITE JACKET!

WHAT WAS ALL THAT COMMOTION, AL?

AAAAH... A SCREW-BALL IF I EVER SAW ONE. DEMONS WE HAVE TO WORRY ABOUT NOW.

THAT NIGHT...

HOW'D YOUR DAY GO, AL?

FORGET MY DAY. HOW'S LITTLE JOHNNY?

HI, YAH, DAD! WHAT'D YOU BRING FOR ME?

A PRETZEL... A WHISTLE...

...AND A BIG HUG!

I SHOULD BE JEALOUS, AL. YOU NEVER HUG ME THAT WAY!

NEXT MORNING. THAT'S AL'S HOUSE AGAIN... YOU GUESSED IT...HE'S AT THE BREAKFAST TABLE, FLIPPING THROUGH THE NEWSPAPER...

AL! WHAT'S WRONG?! WHAT DID YOU JUST READ IN THE NEWSPAPER?

WOMAN CRUSHED BY FALLING CORNICE

MISS HERMIONE LAURENTS, WELL-KNOWN DABBLER IN THE OCCULT, WAS KILLED YESTERDAY AFTERNOON OUTSIDE A DAY NURSE...

AL, YOU'RE SO PALE...WHAT'S WRONG?

C-COULD SHE HAVE BEEN GIVING ME THE RIGHT DOPE? INNOCENT-LOOKING CHILDREN ...DAY NURSERY. MAYBE THEY FOUND OUT SHE WAS TRYING TO STOOL ON THEM! MAYBE THEY KILLED HER!

NO! SHE WAS NUTS! HER DEATH WAS AN ACCIDENT! NOTHING BUT AN ACCIDENT!

AL, YOU'RE JUST SITTING THERE SAYING NOTHING! BUT SOMETHING'S WRONG... I CAN TELL! PLEASE, AL, TELL ME WHAT'S WRONG!

AL,...THAT LOOK ON YOUR FACE! WH-WHERE ARE YOU GOING?

STAY DOWN HERE TIL I CALL YOU, CLARA. DON'T COME IN TIL I CALL.

I'M GOING TO JOHNNY'S ROOM...TO SEE IF HE'S ALL RIGHT!

I MUST'VE BEEN CRAZY TO COME UP HERE. THAT DAME WAS NUTS. I-I JUST DID THIS OUT OF RESPECT, SORT OF, TO HER MEMORY. HMMM ...DARK IN HERE. I'LL PULL UP THE SHADE...

THERE! NOW I CAN REALLY SEE...

JOHNNY IS ONE OF THEM! JOHNNY IS ONE OF THE DEMONS!

"THEY HAVE RENDERED THEMSELVES VULNERABLE.. IF JUST ONE OF THEM IS RECOGNIZED, AND IMMEDIATELY KILLED, ALL OF THEM WILL PERISH..."

"IT WORKS EVERY TIME! EVERY TIME I FEEL BLUE, ALL I HAVE TO DO IS TAKE A PEEK AT JOHNNY, AND I'M WALKING ON CLOUDS AGAIN..."

"BUT IF ON THE OTHER HAND, ONE IS RECOGNIZED AND NOT KILLED, THEN BY THE SAME TOKEN, THE WORLD WILL BE THEIRS BY DEFAULT..."

"WHEN I THINK OF THOSE EIGHTEEN YEARS WITHOUT A KID..."

"YOU WILL KNOW INSIDE! A VOICE INSIDE YOUR HEART WILL TELL YOU..."

AL, I COULDN'T WAIT ANY LONGER! I'M SCARED...AL, WHATS THE GUN IN YOUR HAND FOR? AL, WHAT'RE YOU GOING TO DO?!

I DON'T KNOW, CLARA! ... I (SOB) ... DON'T KNOW?

IF YOU WERE AL, WHAT WOULD YOU DO?

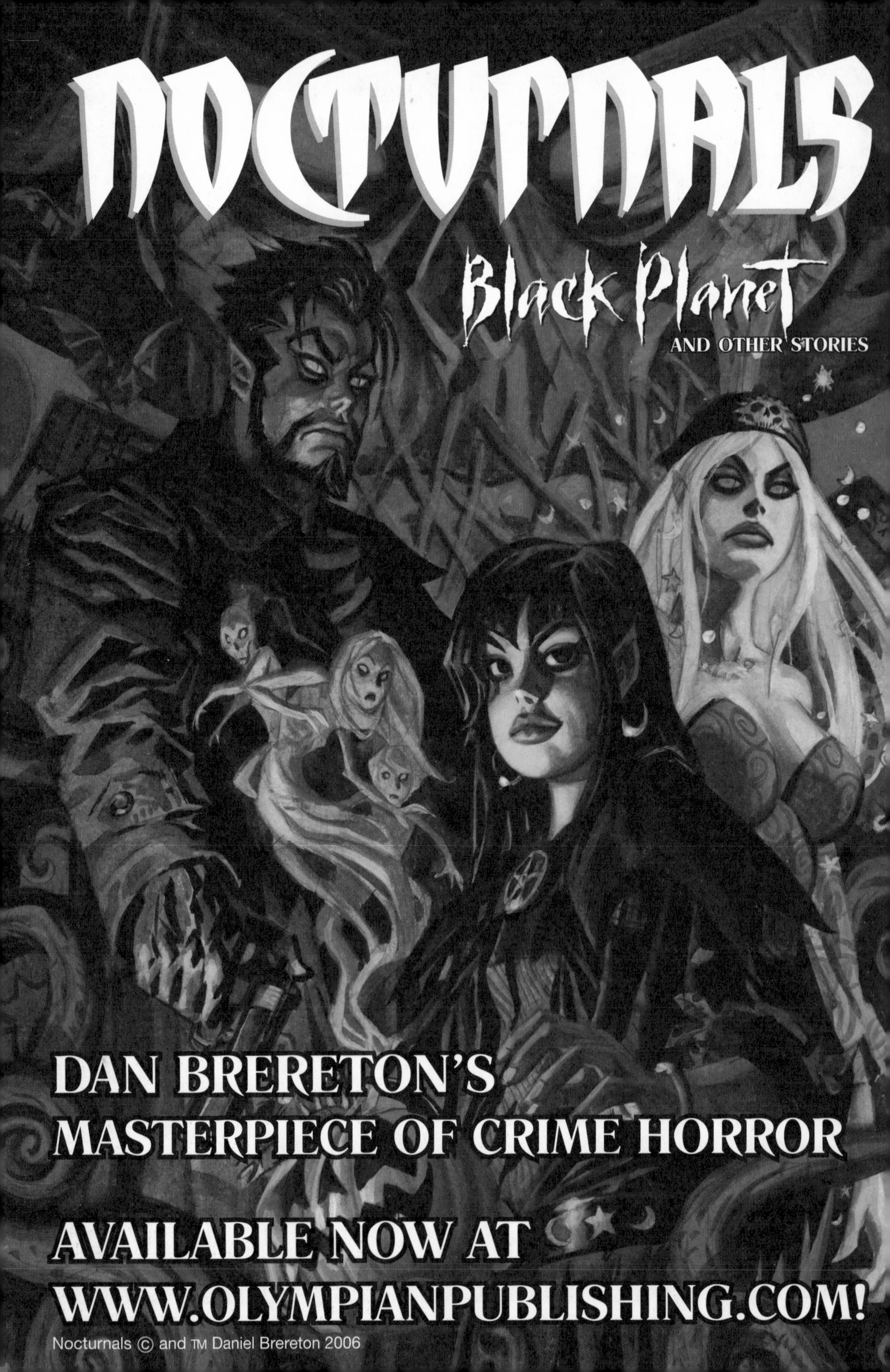
NOCTURNALS
Black Planet
AND OTHER STORIES
DAN BRERETON'S
MASTERPIECE OF CRIME HORROR
AVAILABLE NOW AT
WWW.OLYMPIANPUBLISHING.COM!
Nocturnals © and ™ Daniel Brereton 2006